Hospital Days

Reminiscence of a Civil War Nurse

by

Jane Stuart Woolsey

*with an introduction
by Daniel John Hoisington*

Edinborough Press

Printed in the United States of America by Thomson-Shore, Inc.
Typeface: ITC New Baskerville
Research Associate: Daniel Aaron Hoisington

Cover Art: "Heroes and Heroines of the Civil War," by Thomas Nast. Harper's Weekly, April 9, 1864.

Publisher's Cataloguing–in–Publication Data
Woolsey, Jane Stuart.
   Hospital Days: Reminiscence of a Civil War Nurse.
   Edited with an introduction by Daniel John Hoisington.
   ISBN 1-889020-00-1
   1. United States–History–Civil War, 1861-1865–Personal narratives;
   2. United States–History–Civil War, 1861-1865–Hospitals.
   3. United States–History–Civil War, 1861-1865–Women.
   I. Woolsey, Jane Stuart. II. Hoisington, Daniel John. III. Title.

E621.W87 1996   96-84320
973.7'76–dc20   LCCN

Contents

Jane Stuart Woolsey

Hospital Days

Introduction

J ANE STUART WOOLSEY was one of the thousands of women who served in military hospitals during the Civil War. Woolsey came from a remarkable family with the mother, seven sisters, and one brother contributing to the Union cause. After the war, three sisters—Jane, Georgeanna and Abby—remained active in the nursing profession.

Jane, the second daughter of Charles and Jane Eliza Woolsey, was born on a ship off the coast of Connecticut in 1830. In 1840 her father died, leaving nine children. The widow and her family lived in relative comfort in New York City, supported by relatives and inheritances. As the children came of age, they became immersed in the political upheaval that led to the outbreak of war. As her sister wrote, "When the members of the Woolsey family gave up toys, they took up politics. Brought up by a mother who hated slavery, although her ancestors for generations had been Virginia slave-holders, they walked with her in the straight path of abolitionism."

After the attack on Fort Sumter, the family looked for ways to support the war for the Union. The women, barred from military service, turned to a developing network of civilian organizations created to aide the war effort. They were fortunate that New York City was a hot bed for these groups. They participated in the first meetings of the Women's Central Relief Association, precursor to the U.S. Sanitary Commission, directed by a fellow New Yorker, Frederick Law Olmsted.

Georgeanna Woolsey, one of Jane's sisters, joined the nursing volunteers at once. Dorothea Dix established careful rules for the volunteers. As Georgeanna described them to her family, "First, one must be so old, and no older; have eyes and a nose and a mouth expressing such traits, and no others; must be willing to scrub floors, if necessary." Although, to Dix, the acceptable age was thirty, Georgeanna was twenty-eight. Jane, with typical wit, told a friend, "Society just now presents the unprecedented spectacle of many women trying to make believe that they are over thirty!"[1]

Georgeanna Woolsey ("G.") had a distinguished career in nursing after the Civil War.

Dix established guidelines for appropriate clothing. "Georgy" gathered a simple wardrobe, including two gray cotton cross-grained skirts, two Zouave jackets, four white aprons with waists and large pockets, two washable petticoats to take the place of a hoop and "a nice long flannel dressing gown which may be put on in a hurry and fly out if the city is bombarded or anything else." She had one dress made of black gabardine and a black neopolitan straw bonnet trimmed with green ribbon. The rest of the kit included towels, sheets, soap, cologne, oil silk, sponges, a small camp cooking stove, and a spirit lamp.[2]

Georgeanna traveled to Washington, D.C. to serve under Dix. The work, physically strenuous, was made more difficult by the social barriers to the nurses. The established surgeons objected to the presence of women in the wards. Georgeanna wrote, "No one knows, who did not watch the thing from the beginning, how much opposition, how much ill-will, how much unfeeling want of thought these women nurses endured...Government had determined that women should be employed, and the army surgeons determined to make their lives so unbearable that they would be forced in self-defense to leave." The women were further handicapped by a general disorganization in the training, assignment, and daily supervision of the nurses. [3]

Jane Woolsey remained in New York City during 1861 and 1862, helping the Women's Central Association and visiting the local hospitals as part of the Woman's Auxiliary Committee. In January 1863 Georgy accepted a new assignment on the staff at the Army Hospital in Portsmouth Grove, Rhode Island. Jane joined her to become assistant superintendents under Katherine Wormeley. With Wormeley and Georgeanna as her mentors, Jane learned hospital management.[4]

In the fall of 1863, Jane was ready for a larger mission. The Army changed Portsmouth Grove to a prison hospital, leaving the two sisters in search of other work. Georgeanna described the circumstances:

> It was suggested to Mrs. Gibbons...that there was work to be done at the large barrack hospital established on the Fairfax Theological Seminary grounds near Alexandria; and through Mrs. Gibbons, an introduction was secured for us to the surgeon, Dr. David Page Smith, who called to talk matters over with us. We followed up the conversation with an inspection of the hospital, and were put through a catechism by Dr. Smith as to what we thought we could do, if we came and took charge. The result was that he told us he should like us to try it, and we moved over the river and were installed as Superintendents of nursing, and quartered in the house of the Chaplain and his wife. [5]

The Woolsey sisters took up the task of creating a system for the Alexandria hospital. Georgeanna Woolsey wrote, "Jane and I found ourselves in absolute control of our own department, and most cordially sustained by the surgeon-in-charge." His support was essential. By 1863 the power to appoint nurses was shifted away from Dorothea Dix to the hospital surgeons. The Woolseys agreed with this move, as Georgeanna noted, "Miss Dix has a standing misunderstanding with the Surgeon in Charge; in short, she hates him. He is a genius; a remarkable man in his profession." Jane dedicated *Hospital Days* to Dr. Smith.[6]

Her new post was an important position. Jane's mother described a visit: "I looked into her poorly furnished little bedroom, which seemed to me very bare, and very unsuited

to Jane's ideas and tastes, but which she seems perfectly contented and happy with. It is a fine building, airy and beauti-
fully situated, very clean, and everything about it in perfect
order, and Jane the supreme directress. It was strange, indeed,
to see her there, all alone, and hundreds of men waiting for
their portion at her hands."[7]

That "fine building" was located on the grounds of the
Fairfax Episcopal Seminary, one of the most prestigious theological schools in the South. Among its graduates were Phillips
Brooks, Bishop William Meade and Bishop Henry Whipple.
When the war came, they dismissed classes and abandoned
the grounds. Classes would meet in Staunton, Virginia
throughout the rest of the war. [8] The Yankees' occupation
offended many Virginians. Frank Jones, a Virginia soldier,
climbed on a nearby hill in September 1861, writing home:

The Virginia Theological Seminary

You could see the tall spire of the Seminary building and a large U.S. flag waiving over Fort Albany or Ellsworth just this side of the Seminary, this is an immense earthwork where they have mounted heavy guns, how dare the vandals to occupy those grounds I love so well...O how long will the enemies of our country be allowed to tread upon our soil & desecrate our holy places! [9]

The Southern Churchman, an influential religious journal, printed a description of a visit to the grounds in mid-1862. "Approaching the Seminary from the rear, we found the country so much altered that we could scarcely recognize it. All the trees for miles in the rear of the seminary have been cut down. We found the Seminary building used as a hospital; more than two hundred sick were in it." A later story, run in the fall of 1863, assured its readers that the sacred ground was safe. A correspondent for the *Alexandria News* reported, "Notwithstanding the large number of troops all the time quartered in this vicinity or passing through and that it has been and still is occupied as a hospital, everything is in handsome order."[10]

Woolsey brought a gift for management to her work. "Was the system of women–nurses in hospitals a failure?" Woolsey asks in *Hospital Days*. "There never was any system." Women came as volunteers, family relations, or military employees. The Civil War nurse, as described in *Hospital Days*, provided support rather than medical skill. They assisted with an elaborate "special diet" system that served as primary care and a topic to which Woolsey gives considerable discussion. The nurses wrote letters for soldiers and acted as intermediary for families. Jane Woolsey, as director of the nurses, managed distribution of supplies sent by the U.S. Sanitary Commission.

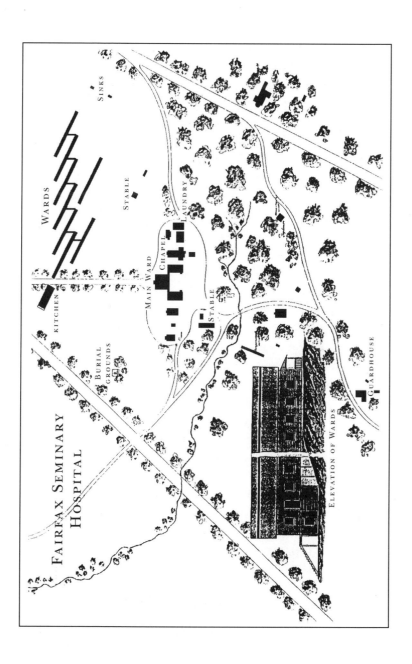

FAIRFAX SEMINARY HOSPITAL

Recollections of Jane Woolsey's service tell of a compassionate nurse. Her sister remembered, "You should have seen her with her bonnet off, her camel's hair shawl swung gracefully from her shoulders and a great-pocketed white apron on, making tea over a spirit lamp and enjoying it all so thoroughly." The Rev. Henry Hopkins, a chaplain at the hospital, wrote many years later, "No picture from any scene of my life is more vivid in my recollection than that of Jane, of beloved memory, as I saw her sometimes at Fairfax—her illuminated face with the wonderful eyes, and the wonderful smile, her fragile form wrapped in the ermine-lined cloak she used to wear." [11] The descriptions of her clothing suggest that the strict rules of Dorothea Dix were bent in later years.

Georgeanna left the Alexandria hospital in May 1864, traveling to Fredericksburg to assist with hospital transports. Jane reprinted several of her sister's letters from that period in *Hospital Days*. Georgeanna finished her war service at the Beverly, New Jersey hospital. Jane Woolsey remained at the Fairfax Seminary until the hospital closed in August 1865. Many buildings decribed in her book are still standing and are listed on the National Register of Historic Places. [12]

She returned to New York and wrote her book. *Hospital Days* provides one of the best descriptions of the day-to-day work of the nurses. Always intended for the family, the Woolseys printed only one hundred copies in 1868 with a small reprint in 1870. Although it was not widely read, the *New York Evening Post* called the preface, "...one of the most perfect bits of English prose within our knowledge."[13] Woolsey was a good writer with an eye for a story and that quality sets this reminiscence apart from many similar books.

With experience and management skills from her Civil War service, Woolsey looked for a new avenue for her talents.

She returned to Virginia for four years, working at the Hampton Normal and Agricultural Institute, a school established by the Freedman's Bureau. At the Hampton Institute Woolsey supervised the "girl's industries" including sewing and housework classes.

Woolsey took the position of resident director at New York Presbyterian Hospital in 1872, working with her sister, Abby. The job gave her considerable authority, described by a historian as equivalent to an executive vice president. Her power created dissension among many of the male physicians who resented a woman being given such wide responsibilities. After one confrontation in 1875, several of those doctors were replaced by the hospital's board. Woolsey kept up her literary efforts during this time, submitting numerous articles to the local newspapers. She suffered from ill health following a bout with rheumatic fever in the early 1870s and resigned her hospital position in 1876. Jane remained an invalid for the rest of her life, cared for by her sister, Abby Woolsey. She died in 1891.[14]

I am indebted to Anne Austin, *The Woolsey Sisters of New York: A Family's Involvement in the Civil War and a New Profession* (Philadelphia: American Philosophical Society, 1971).

[1] Georgeanna Woolsey Bacon, *Letters of a Family during the War for the Union, 1861-1865* (New Haven: Tuttle, Morehouse and Taylor, 1899), pp. 79-82.

[2] Bacon, *Letters*, pp. 106-107.

[3] Bacon, *Letters*, p. 145-146.

[4] Bacon, *Letters*, pp. 479-534. Also see Katherine Prescott Wormeley, *The Cruel Side of the War* (Boston: Roberts, 1898).

[5] Bacon, *Letters*, p. 551.

[6] *Letter*s, pp. 558-559; see David Gollaher, *Voice for the Mad: The Life of Dorothea Dix* (New York: The Free Press, 1995), pp. 416-419.

[7] Bacon, *Letters*, p. 709.

[8] Rev. William A. R. Goodwin, *History of the Theological Seminary in Virginia and Its Historical Background* (New York: Edwin S. Gorham, 1923).

[9] Margaretta Barton Colt, *Defend the Valley: A Shenandoah Family in the Civil War* (New York: Orion Books, 1994), p. 100.

[10] *The Southern Churchman,* July 4, 1862; Nov. 6, 1863.

[11] Bacon, *Letters*, p. 559.

[12] National Register of Historic Places Nomination Form.

[13] *New York Evening Post,* May 30, 1893.

[14] Austin, pp. 123-129; Dr. Albert Lamb, *The Presbyterian Hospital and the Columbia Medical Center, 1868–1943* (New York: Columbia University Press, 1955), p. 19.

To

The "Surgeon in Charge,"

Honored Commander,
True Comrade,
Beloved Friend,

This Little Story of the Hospital is Inscribed.

I N THE AUTUMN OF 1865, when the new Peace on all the hills and fields made them seem so sweet and fair, we found ourselves, a family long parted, exploring the by-roads in the north New Hampshire country. Following, one day, a winding green wagon-track, far from the main road, we came upon a desolate rough farm half way up the lower slopes of the Bartlett mountain. A dozen sheep were scattered over the stony fields, and among them sat a man in the full uniform of a Zouave, bagging trowsers, gay-braided jacket, cap, tassel, and long bright crimson scarf, complete. He had but just got home from some distant post, with very little back pay in his pocket for the sick wife, and none at all to spend in sober clothes, and had gone at once to work upon the obstinate farm, all in his gay attire. He seemed a little stunned by the silence round him. He "missed the drums," he said. We had a little talk over the old days already so distant although so near, and left him, the sun touching the red and the blue of his bright garments, tending his sheep under the solemn hills.

One who sits and listens for the drums to-day seems like the Zouave among the sheep-crofts; the flags and the music have marched so far away. And yet there may be some, in these times of gain-getting, pleasure-seeking, and "reaction" who are not sorry to look backward a little, now and then, and refresh from the old fountains their courage and their love of country.

First Days

O N A BLUE-AND-GOLD DAY in the edge of November, a hundred years ago, two ladies, with their luggage, were carefully packed into an ambulance, the conveyance of the period, at the door of a great city hotel. They were setting out—with an easy and cheerful-minded confidence in the unknown, which seems strange to them as they look back at it, but which must have been part of the spirit of the time— for a lonely outpost hospital to which they had been invited by the officer in charge, as supervisors of the nursing and cooking department.

Through the unclean paste of the city streets; over a long bridge and a turbid river, hindered by endless wagon-trains, halted by German sentinels, who read the passes upside down; along roads in which the heavy wheels turned back the soft soil as a plough turns the loam in the fields; through little sparkling streams that rushed across the carriage-way; by miles and miles of treeless, open, desolate country—fields on fields—full of deep-red dwarf oaks, and low, thick, yellow shrubbery—in the smoky sunshine and sweet, spicy air; at last, climbing by long slopes a pleasant height, they came to the grove skirting the Hospital grounds, and wound up to the brick rear-court of a large quadrangle of buildings.

The officer in charge came out to meet them, and took them over to their lodgings in the parsonage, a few yards from the central offices. They were so fortunate as to be assigned quarters in the house with the Chaplain and his family, and were shown into a large octagon-sided room, with bare, clean floor, two camp beds, with bed-sacks stuffed with straw, two little tables with regulation tin basins, and in the wide fire-place a huge black cylinder of sheet-iron, giving out a dull roar, and growing red here and there in spots.

Out of the windows lay the sweetest country. Just under them were the remnants of a garden—lilac, syringa, and straggling bushes on which two or three late, pale roses fluttered and hung. These stood up to their knees in the long, rough grass, and the grass covered the rolling ground down to the feathery edge of trees and the deepcut, yellow cross-roads. Beyond the road the red fields reached far away, and beyond the fields, curving and shining, moved the river. A streak of mist, and a steeple here and there, showed where the nearest town grovelled along the river's edge; and on the left, looking through miles of airy purple, hung in the smoke of the city, and the autumn vapor, a wonderful white dome, not yet lifting aloft, nor having the right to lift the finished figure of Liberty. Months and years made every gleam and shadow, every color and line of the landscape dear and familiar to the two who looked out upon it delighted, on the first day of their new life.

The Hospital was a divinity school in the old days, but very early in the war-time professors and pupils fled away southward, in such unseemly haste to declare for the rebellion that doors were left ajar, women's gowns hanging in the cupboards, books lying open, face downwards, on the tables. One of the first cares of the Surgeon in Charge was to have all these books collected, carefully boxed, and sent to the nearest provost-marshal for safe keeping. The deserted buildings first fell into the hands of brigade and division commanders, were occupied as headquarters for a few months, and were then set apart for General Hospital uses.

The beautiful grove was spared by special order. The brick and stone buildings scattered through it, dormitories, class–halls, professors' houses, library and chapel, with the addition of a little village of barracks, made excellent accommodation for the sick. The ground falls away from this pleasant height on all sides but the south. Southward the brown waste stretches unbroken; no fence, no tree; wide, desolate, but sweet; dipping here and there into ravines full of mist and soft color; climbing at last against the sky in other heights, where, for many months, rebels came and went at their pleasure, making strong their offensive defences, and flaunting their insolent banner.

Special Diet

O N THE MORNING AFTER their arrival, the new-comers, who had already been formally mustered into the service of the United States, were put on duty in published orders, and were waited on in the store-room bay the women-nurses in a body, somewhat prepared to resent if occasion offered, but soon melting and smiling on observing the unformidable aspect of the new authority. "Them dear lambs!" said old Mrs. B., afterwards, "what *I* was afraid of was caps."

The store-room was a comfortable room in the central or Administration building, over the main entrance, with the luxury of an open wood fire and a wide window overlooking the barracks and the lovely view. Down the sides of this room ran shelves and cupboards for storing all manner of comforts; regulation supplies proper to the Special Diet department, and outside gifts of all kinds which began to flow in at once, and continued flowing in a twice-blessed current all the days of the service. To this store-room was afterwards added a much larger room next door, nicely fitted up and bountifully filled with good things.

An exploration was then made of every nook and corner of the Hospital. A little ripple of smiles followed the Surgeon in Charge up and down the wards, and the men to whom he spoke or whom he touched, loosening or righting strap or bandage, looked proud and pleased.

In the course of this tour of inspection the Superintendent received a few words of instruction as to her position and its duties. She might visit in the wards, distribute little extra comforts, talk with the men, write letters and "sympathize" as much as she had time and inclination for, but her serious business was to see that the women-nurses did their duty, and that the Special Diet was everything that it ought to be. She was required to know what quantity and quality of raw material was furnished by the commissary steward; to see that this was properly cooked, properly distributed from the diet kitchen, received in good order in the wards, carefully divided there; that each patient got, without unlawful leakage, the exact articles ordered for him by the ward medical officer; in short, she was expected to follow the food from the commissary storehouse down the sick man's throat.

To these duties the Superintendent added in her own mind, among others, that of learning whether the permitted articles were cooked according to the taste and fancy of the individual, knowing well that A prefers salt and B sugar in the same kind of porridge, and disliking from her soul the tall-men-powders-short-men-pills system she has observed elsewhere.

A chief special diet cook and five or six assistants were detailed for the kitchen, and a set of printed forms and tables arranged by which everything was made methodic and easy. "Call my attention to any roughness you see in the working of this or that order," said the Surgeon in Charge. "Observe,

observe continually; your observation is worth more than my theory."

Standing where she could see and sympathize with the "difficulties and scruples of authority," as well as with the needs and helplessness of suffering, the Superintendent eagerly availed herself of the privileges of her position. The diet system was from time to time altered and improved, until a set of tables, blanks, and orders was fixed on, so "fitly framed together" that the little department moved, without undue friction, fairly and smoothly to the end.

The Surgeon in Charge made the diet system the subject of much thought, observation, and care. "We must have order and economy," he said, "but we must also avoid all restriction in gratifying the lawful wants of the sick. The Hospital fund is to be used, as far as possible, for the very men out of whose rations it is saved." He declared that patients and their needs could be classified to a great extent; that it was safer on all sides to use, in the large proportion of cases, a set of fixed bills of fare specifying the proper dishes for each meal, rather than a miscellaneous list of articles from which inexperienced ward officer and captious patient should make up together their programme of a harmonious banquet. The Superintendent has in her possession many original orders on the diet kitchen, of which the following are specimens:

Private H. (Inflammation of stomach) Hot cakes, cheese and molasses candy.

Private C. (Chronic diarrhœa.) Grated flour porridge, lemonade, oyster soup, oatmeal gruel and peppermint tea.

Private J. (Chronic diarrhœa.)

BREAKFAST	DINNER	SUPPER
Coffee	Roast Beef	Oyster Soup
Steak	Fish	Raw Cabbage
Eggs	Radishes	Cheese
Bread	Boiled Cabbage	Bread
Butter	Bread	Butter
Milk-punch	Tea	Coffee

Private K. (Typhoid fever.)

BREAKFAST	DINNER	SUPPER
Mutton Chops	Beefsteak	Milk
Potatoes	Potatoes	Tea
Bread	Tea	Arrowroot
Coffee	Coffee	Cake
Doughnuts	Butter	Butter
Butter	Plum Pudding	Pudding

The Surgeon in Charge held that a roast beef and pudding diet, an eggs and milk diet, a vegetable diet for men touched with scurvy, a milk-porridge diet, a beef-tea diet, and a gruel diet, would cover the majority of cases; one entire table being changed for another as it stood, as often as was necessary for variety; for the most delicate food given monotonously disgusts the sick person. Private Davidson, Ward D, for instance, was very fond of chicken stewed in rice, and a nice dish of it was prepared for him. The ward surgeon neglected or forgot to make a change in the diet order, and the chicken was duly sent day after day, until Private D. became so exasperated with the sight and even the smell of it, that weeks afterward when the same dish was brought for his next neighbor, he seized a moment when his comrades back was turned, crawled from his bed and threw the whole mess, dish and all, out of the window.

The Surgeon in Charge thought it necessary, however, to leave some liberty, outside of all fixed tables, as the sick man's appetite sometimes requires tempting, not only with frequent changes, but with "home dishes" and dishes prepared to some extent after his own fancy. Badly wounded men, too, often consume almost unlimited quantities of food and stimulants. For all such cases special blanks were provided, on which any and all reasonable articles might be ordered by the ward surgeon. A little book of the gravest cases was kept in the storeroom, and constant note taken of their needs and progress. The incessant, strenuous effort of the Surgeon in Charge was, to put it in a grand way, to make

"Perfect law commeasure perfect freedom."

The framework of the diet system is this:

First. The Diet Table, a bill of fare or fixed carte drawn up by the Surgeon in Charge, prescribing the different articles for each meal, under several general heads, with the exact quantity of each man's ration, in pounds, ounces, pints, etc., set down in the margin, thus:

Private Jones, No. l, is ordered by his ward surgeon "Eggs and Milk Diet." Referring from the return to the diet tables posted in the store-room and in all the wards, we see that "Eggs and Milk Diet" means that Private Jones is to have for:

BREAKFAST	DINNER	SUPPER
Milk 1 pint	Milk 1 pint	Milk 1 pint
Eggs poached, No. 2	Chicken 8 oz.	Milk toast 6 oz.
Milk Toast 6 oz.	Custard 6 oz.	Butter 1 oz.
Butter 1 oz.	Bread 4 oz.	Cheese 1 oz.

Second. The Ward Diet blank, or Return, in which every man's needs for the day are entered under his name and number. Private Jones, No. 1, Eggs and Milk Diet. Private Robinson, No. 2, Beef-tea Diet. One of these returns for each ward comes to the Superintendent every day in the morning.

Third. The Ward Returns aggregated by the Superintendent on one blank for the kitchen.

Fourth. The Requisition on the commissary steward for the raw material; so many pounds, ounces, quarts, etc., based on the aggregate returns.

This, for instance, is a copy of the Requisition on the commissary steward for May 22, 1865, the number of patients on the Special Diet returns for that day being 346:

"The commissary steward will please issue for Special Diet:

Bread	390 lbs.
Butter	40 lbs.
Milk	350 qts.
Beef	130 lbs.
Chickens	(11 pair) 22
Potatoes	125 lbs.

```
Onions........................................ 30 lbs.
Sugar..........................................30 lbs.
Coffee.......................................10  lbs.
Pickles....................................... 4 qts.
Rice...........................................15 lbs.
Dried apples............................... 15 lbs.
Salt........................................... 7 lbs.
Oysters .................................. 4 gallons
```

Signed by the Superintendent."

The lighter supplies, tea, loaf-sugar, eggs, dried beef, corn-starch, etc.; tomatoes, cheese, fresh butter, sweetmeats, spices and wines, are issued from the store-room, and an account is kept in the store-room Book of Issues. Voluntary supplies for general distribution are stored and issued in the same way.

Fifth. The commissary steward's daily evening report, a dupli-cate of which is sent to the Superintendent. This shows the quantity of all raw material received, issued, and remaining on hand in the commissary storehouse.

Sixth. The order on the grocer or tradesman in the town, of which blanks signed by the Surgeon in Charge are furnished the Superintendent to be filled up by her with the extra ar-ticles needed, not issued by either commissary or medical purveyor, but to be bought out of the hospital fund.

These papers check each other; the Superintendent is re-quired to keep copies of them all on file. At the end of the month the tradesmen's bills are sent to her to compare with the retained copies of the orders, when mistakes or fraud are easily detected. "But no theory is perfect," said the Surgeon in Charge, in one of his short lay sermons; "no system can be framed to exclude dishonesty. Eternal vigilance is the price of special diet. Inspect, inspect without ceasing."

All mixed drinks, *i.e.*, punches, egg-nog, mulled wine, wine-whey, lemonade, and acid fruit-drinks and sherbets, are prepared by the Superintendent, and issued when called for.

In order that the occasional extra resources of the Hospital, or the gifts of friends, might be used with judgment and impartiality, the Surgeon in Charge had a little type-holder and printer's pad provided, with which the Superintendent could fill in blank spaces in the diet returns. The steward announced, let us do him the justice to say, with evident pleasure, "You can draw on the garden for green peas to-day, about so many bushels." The tipsy, but benevolent corporal in the printing-office, was always delighted to set up and the Superintendent to stamp on a lot of ward returns the charming words, green peas, or canned peaches, fresh fish, strawberries, corn-cake, tomatoes, tomato-omelettes, string-beans, etc., etc., and send the blanks round to all the wards. The ward officers could then fill in names and numbers as they liked, and there was not much danger of improper or unequal distribution.

Superintendent's Day

THE OUTLINE OF A SUPERINTENDENT'S DAY, with digressions, is like this; and all days—week days, Sundays, and holidays—are very much alike.

Soon after breakfast, provided for over night, the ward returns begin to come in. A little rattle in the tin post-office box on the store-room door; Ward A is early to-day; so much the better. It happened to the writer, visiting elsewhere and wanting to speak to the ward surgeon, to ask, "At what time does Dr. B. make his rounds?" "Well 'm," answered the wardmaster, "that depends on *how* drunk he was the night before." One after another the returns come in; A, B, C, D, E, F, G, H, I, E, L, M, N, O, P, Q; sixteen of them today. They are aggregated on one sheet, quantities are estimated, and the requisition on the commissary steward made out. Supplies necessary from the Superintendent's store-room are estimated, and amounts entered in the store-room book. The stimulants are prepared and issued. The punches are compounded in huge caldrons with stopcocks and drawn off into armies of ward bottles. Each man's bottle is carefully re-washed before filling (ward bottle-washing not recognized), corked and re-labelled with adhesive label with his name and number. The bottles are carried in butler's boxes to the wards and delivered to the women-nurses, through whom the special diet and extra delicacies of all sorts are distributed.

It is time now and over-time to go to the kitchen and give directions about dinner. The kitchen is a very large, light basement room, under the Administration building. The two chief conditions of efficiency in the special diet service are a good central kitchen and rapid communication with all parts of the Hospital. The fixtures and utensils of the kitchen are abundant and of the best quality. Recipes, either regulation or modifications of Dutch and New England master-pieces, are plainly written out and posted on the walls in perpetual sight; how to poach eggs; beef-tea, one ration; chicken soup, one ration; corn bread, one ration. Every dish is inspected or tasted. The Superintendent confesses to a furtive silver spoon in the pocket of her apron. The main articles of food are, of course, prepared in bulk in large vessels, and measuring cans and ladles of various sizes hang in shining ranks against the walls. John is justly proud of his tin-scouring.

Down one side of the kitchen runs a long dresser or table. Here are ranged in order the sliding shelves or trays of the diet wagon: A, a; B, b; C, c; D, E, and F; one or more for each ward. Hung on the wall, over the table, is the aggregated list; the "aggravated return," John calls it, as if it were a kind of sickness. By long practice we all know to an invisible fraction how much is one ration, and how much ten or twenty rations of anything. If difference of opinion arises we weigh again. All fluids are carefully measured in cans of exact capacity. The great wooden ladles hold so many ounces of mashed potato and so many of custard, etc. The covered cans, dishes, and jugs are set quickly on the trays and quickly filled. It is wonderful how rapidly this can be done with division of labor and practice. The trays are shoved through the long windows and lifted into the compartments of the wagon; the doors of the wagon are buttoned to, and with the "double teamed" in blue and a guard behind, it sets out swiftly and smoothly along the railed plank-walk or tramway which runs all over the camp. The car halts in front of each ward; the wardroom window goes up, the trays are passed through, and even at the uttermost barrack the mashed potato hurries in smoking hot. The car makes one or two journeys at every meal, according to the number of men in hospital, and after every meal runs about again and collects and brings in trays, cans, and dishes to be washed in the kitchen. The "wittles train," as the men call it, was somewhat long in coming to full perfection, but, "like the hundred-years flower of the aloe," we said, "this was worth waiting for."

The woman–nurse in each little ward-room receives her tray or trays, having her china plates and cups, her knives and forks and tumblers, set out in order beforehand; divides the food according to a duplicate of the ward return hanging over her table, and the men-nurses carry it about. She follows immediately down the ward, helps and feeds those who are unable to help themselves, and sees that all have enough. If anything goes wrong, she is directed to send word at once to the Superintendent. She has means of heating over any simple thing if the patient does not incline to it at the fixed hour. A sick man will often take his food nicely if he may have his own time about it, and does not feel himself under observation. In critical cases a fresh ration is prepared instead of the *réchauffé*. The small special blanks are meant for these and all other cases of emergency; or the woman-nurse can have anything urgently needed at the moment, by sending her own written request for it. Extra rations of one or two articles—such as beef-tea, oysters, eggs—are always on hand in the kitchen. The Government ration is so generous that when honestly used there is almost always margin enough for extra calls without extra requisitions for raw material. The commissary steward, however, is required by the Surgeon in Charge to keep some trustworthy person in the storehouse ready at all times to fill such requisitions.

The Superintendent follows in the wake of the diet car. Such is the celerity with which the Defenders, even when ill, swallow their food, it is impossible to be in more than one or two wards while eating is actually going on. But by beginning at a different and unexpected ward and meal every day, the objects of an inspection are pretty well secured. "Was the gruel right?" "Did you get a *full* tumbler of punch?" "You are tired of the beef-tea? Grumble as much as you like." "But I don't want to grumble; I aint got no complaints to make—only"— aside to G—— "I'd as lief see the devil coming up the ward as that beef-tea!"

Take a page at random from the Superintendent's shabby, little yellow note-book. What hospital nurse doesn't know the sort? "Cushing complains of the steak; it is too rare."—The Superintendent observes with pain that the Defenders all prefer their steaks cut thin and *fried*.—"Jeffries wants more seasoning in his soup; it is 'too fresh,' he says, and Brooks must have his tomatoes raw, with vinegar. Thompson says the men-nurses are too slow; he says he 'wants particular attention paid to him;' he 'can't eat fish-hash,' and he 'can't eat soup.' Bates wants 'crust coffee,' and explains to me how it should be made. No. 35 hasn't touched his breakfast. 'If he could only have some Boston brown bread.' Mem.: to try and get him some. Eustace is tired of all his drinks; try mulled sherry. Cocoa in F poor and washy to-day. More small cans wanted for gruels.

Ward return wrong—explain to woman-nurse. Quinn running down; try champagne in a long-spouted feeding cup. Mem.: to show nurse in K how to get more dish-towels and hot-water cans for cold feet. Scott says he can't get along without 'jel' for his tea every night. Cut up No. 802's chicken and feed him with it, on his intimation that he will eat it if I do; he admits that it is not as bad as he expected."

After the tour of the wards the chief cook comes for directions, and the tea, sugar, eggs, cheese, etc., for twenty-four hours, are weighed and counted out. The chief cook is an enthusiast in his profession, or rather in his calling, for he was a blacksmith when he enlisted. He came into the Hospital with fever, and, for some inscrutable reason, was, when convalescent, detailed to the diet kitchen. But he "took" at once to his new trade, learned rapidly, and showed great zeal and intelligence in it. His blacksmith's hand was light, accurate, and neat as a woman's. He took genuine pleasure in trying new dishes, and genuine pride in their success. He was often known to follow a nice dish quietly down to the ward, and stand by, enjoying every mouthful the sick man swallowed. He was in "mild misery" if anything failed in flavor or seemed stinted in quantity, and showed real delight when assured that such and such sick men began to mend on good food alone. May fair fortune and fill rations follow him—clear-witted, kind-hearted, faithful Thomas Sullivan, special diet cook.

One day, this note went down in a hurry to the office of the Surgeon in Charge:

"Dear Dr. ——,
"Etc., etc., etc.
"DEAR SIR: Sullivan, chief special diet cook, is ordered to report to the adjutant today before dress parade, and from this time

forth to play upon a drum! Cannot the 'interests of the service' secure him to the kitchen? Surely he is more important there than in the drum corps of this Hospital. Please let him still flourish his wooden Spoons instead of his drum-sticks."

Here is the note officially "returned," endorsed, "Sullivan is restored to his kettles, to remain as long as the Superintendent wishes." There were constant alarms of this kind about the detailed men. "The Hospital subserves the army," said the Surgeon in Charge; "my business is to return every man to the field as soon as possible." So they were swept away. Sometimes entreaty prevailed, as in the case of Sullivan. Later, the organization of an Invalid Corps solved some of these difficulties; but a sorrowful day came when request was made for even the best of the "Invalids" to garrison forts and guard roads, and set the strong regiments free for fighting; and all the good men, clerks, nurses, and cooks, fitted out with various little camp-comforts—headed by Sullivan—marched away under the window of the Superintendent, who waved them a tearful goodbye. Sullivan came to no harm; and many months afterwards, when his corps was at last disbanded, he went home, married his old sweetheart, bought an interest in another blacksmith shop—and the man who can make the best beef-tea in Pennsylvania is pounding his anvil again.

After supplies are issued, and instructions for supper given, there are stores to unpack and arrange, letters to write and answer, applications of all sorts to attend to from patients and nurses, and ward officers who look in to request that this or that article should be sent down to the wards. The women-nurses usually take this time to report special cases and special needs, talk over ward business, and get Sanitary Commission or other outside supplies for the men. The

Sanitary Commission made the Superintendent their representative at the post, and always promptly and generously
filled her requisitions, sending out goods from the nearest
station in their own wagons.

Visitors from the city come in at all times, out of friendship, out of interest, out of curiosity. Some are—how delightful! how refreshing! They lighten the day's work, they make a
bright day brighter, and a dull day bright by their presence,
their silence, and their speech. And some are—how weari-
some! when the addition and subtraction must go on before
them, and they throw the columns into confusion with volleys
of trivial talk; and if you but offer a modest lunch out of a
mess-basket for two, keep calmly asking for clean plates and
tumblers. Then they compel you to go about the wards with
them, and witness the distribution of their little gifts to all the
most unworthy. Sometimes it is a part of old gentlemen, in
civil hats and tumbled, yellow dusters—a Board—for the Hospital is much infested with Boards out of which nothing is
ever builded.

The men come freely, all day long, to the store-room to
"draw," as they call it, tobacco, stationery, games, socks, etc.;
to tell their little stories, and show their home pictures and
letters. It goes to one's heart to hear the clatter of the crutches
on the stair, and the door is never shut except in the hours of
necessary absence. The stream of visitors of this class is almost
unbroken. They are the last before tattoo, and some one is
always waiting, pale and patient, for the opening of the door
in the morning. It makes a little change from the ward for a
convalescent. A soft cracker and a tumbler of some harmless
drink is always ready. How they love these harmless, anonymous drinks! Who does not know the bottle? Short and thick;
twine across the cork—as if the contents were lively! a little

over-leaked in the filling; sawdust sticking to the leaky places; labelled, "Shrub for the soldier, from the East-Hallelujah Aid Society;" a slow, sugary drip-drop, after patient pounding and shaking; this, mixed with water and with a bit of ice in it, "goes jest to the right spot;" this "makes him feel twice the man he was when he come up the stairs."

Then the little rest and talk, and the newspaper or magazine, and some trifle of a "comfort-bag," or pocket-comb, or the like, with the suggestion that the women at home are working and thinking for him, send a poor fellow back to his ward with a little freshness ill his weary day. Many a glimpse of family history we get in this way; many a simple, pathetic story of suffering and unconscious courage; sometimes, very seldom, a wondrous tale—a tale to "make your flesh creep"—of more than human valor and endurance.

Between six and seven the duplicate "commissary steward's evening report" rattles into the tin box on the door. This is taken in, the quantity of stores on hand compared with the probable needs of the next day or two, and the order on the tradesman filled out for the steward's morning journey into town. The records of the day are filed away, the last draughts for the night mixed and sent to the wards, the last inquiries made and charges given concerning the worst cases, and then the slow, sweet bugle calls down rest—blessed rest—upon the camp, and the Superintendent's day, with its digressions, is ended.

Women–Nurses

WAS THE SYSTEM OF WOMEN–NURSES IN HOSPITALS a failure? There never was any system. That the presence of hundreds of individual women as nurses in hospitals was neither an intrusion nor a blunder, let the multitude of their— unsystematized—labors and achievements testify. So far as I know, the experiment of a compact, general organization was never fairly tried. Hospital nurses were of all sorts, and came from various sources of supply; volunteers paid or unpaid; soldiers' wives and sisters who had come to see their friends, and remained without any clear commission or duties; women sent by State agencies and aid societies; women assigned by the General Superintendent of Nurses; sometimes, as in a case I knew of, the wife or daughter of a medical officer drawing the rations, but certainly not doing the work of a "laundress." These women were set adrift in a hospital, eight to twenty of them, for the most part slightly educated, without training or discipline, without company organization or officers, so to speak, of their own, "reporting" to the surgeons, or in the case of persons assigned by her, to the General Superinten- dent, which is very much, in a small way, as if Private Robinson should "report" to General Grant.

There was a standing misunderstanding on the question, for instance, who was authorized to supply women-nurses. An attempt was made, late in 1863, ostensibly to clear up this question. In order No. 351 of the War Department, clause Two says: Women-nurses will be assigned only on application to the General Superintendent, unless, adds clause Three, they are specially appointed by the Surgeon General. Of course, surgeons in charge wishing to retain or employ nurses without the "certificate" of the General Superintendent, applied for their "special appointment" by the Surgeon General, which was promptly obtained. This, with other provisions of the order, practically abolished the office of General Superintendent of Nurses, and threw the selection into the hands of surgeons in charge, which, where the surgeon in charge was an "honest gentleman" and a faithful and efficient officer, was a wise enough measure.

The Roman Catholic system had features which commended it to medical officers of a certain cast of mind. The order and discipline were almost always good. The neatness, etc., were sometimes illusory. There were grave objections to the general introduction of such a system among American volunteer soldiers. There was nothing good in it that we also might not have had; and taking the good, leaving the bad, and adapting the result to the uses of the country and the spirit of the time, we might have had an order of Protestant women better than the Romish "sisterhoods," by so much as heart and intelligence are better than machinery.

A friend, an officer in a neighboring hospital, once wrote to me: "You will be interested to know that we are just now in the midst of a war among the women-nurses, which has continued with varying intensity and fortunes, but with uniform clangor, among changing participants and through different

administrations, since the days of W. and McA. Nevertheless
I stand by the system, convinced that the good which the faithful ones do far outweighs the mischief of the idle and the
tonguey." The last sentence expresses, I think, the general
experience. The whole air and tone of a hospital ward change
and rise after a few days of a woman's presence, and she is an
invaluable auxiliary in the special diet department. Alack!
there be women and women, but let a nurse be ever so obstinate, ignorant, and flabby-minded, she will eagerly, even gaily
starve herself to feed a sick soldier. She may be totally imper-
vious to ideas of order; she may love "hugger-mugger" and
hand-to-mouth ways of getting at objects; she may hopelessly
muddle the ward returns, and interchange sentiment with
the most obnoxious of the stewards, but she will cheerfully
sacrifice time, ease, and health, to the wants or whims of a
wounded man.

Mrs. A—— had "come out," she told me "to *cresh* the rebellion," which she conceived she could best do by distributing inordinate quantities of what she called "sanitary jel." She
had a difference with Mrs. C——, who considered the pickled cucumber the proper weapon against the enemies of the
country, and with Miss L—— who, absorbed in her great
Project of Pin-cushions for the ward, and illuminated mot-
toes for the Entire Hospital, never knew when the air was foul
and the beef-tea glazing at the edges.

Mrs. M—— announced with dignity, at our first interview:
"I am a Daughter of Pennsylvania. You must have heard of
Curtin's Daughters? I have been in the field with the ——
brigade, in such and such battles and such and such skirmishes.
All this may be found in my journal." Then, after a little conversation, she revealed that she had given us the "sign" or
pass-word of two or three orders, and as none had been "taken

up," she inferred we "was all right." She had registered a vow not to serve with any "Sisters," or with members of any secret society. She gave also the details of an interview with the General Superintendent, who had visited the Hospital not long before. The nurse-corps paraded. "And when she came to me," said the child of the Keystone State—"she looked hard at me, and says she, 'So you're the regiment woman!' at which I drew myself up and looking back at her as good as she sent, says I, 'No, madam,' says I; 'I am not the regiment woman, I am the *brigade* woman!'" Whether the new administration was disappointing or fresh fields of laurel unfolded elsewhere, I do not know, but in a few weeks "letters requiring her presence at home" arrived, and the Daughter of Pennsylvania was seen no more.

Miss D—— was an excellent little creature, gentle-mannered, delicate, tremulous, full of intense and indignant patriotism. Night and day found her unflagging in her place. Watch had to be kept over her lest she should never get proper food or rest. She could not work by rule or method. She lost the law in the exceptions. She took what she thought "short cuts," and hand-to-mouth ways of doing what systematic effort would have accomplished in half the time. She was full of goodness and devotion. When she was not at a patient's pillow she was hurrying eagerly to the storeroom to collect comforts and tell the abuses and atrocities she had seen. She thought all military restriction atrocious. She wanted "to go and see Mr. Lincoln about it." Her health gave way before the end of the war and she went home. We were very sorry to part with her. I am afraid the generous heart that beat so fast is scarcely beating now.

Mrs. H——, wife of the commissary sergeant, one of the most capable and faithful of our men, had a placid, sweet face, that might do a sick man good to look on. Her dress was simple and fresh, her voice, even her manner, quiet and soothing. She had a fever while she was at the hospital, and was too delicate to do much service in nursing; but it was comfortable to know that she was moving about the ward, restraining roughness by her gentle presence, and overlooking the distribution of the food and stimulants.

Miss S—— was a German who had followed a relative to the Hospital, and asked for employment as a nurse. She had her virtues and her uses, chief of which was interpreting between the ward surgeon and the German patients. She was a famous knitter of nice woollen socks. She supplied and repaired the whole ward. But she could not resist feeding her "browthers" clandestinely, with the delicacies of their native land, made in the nurses' mess kitchen. One of these was a warm and washy beverage called "beer-soup," and another was an anonymous mixture of something like glue, cabbage, and pot-scrapings. We rather winked at the beer-soup, for beer in any shape is such a comfort to the brave Teuton, but the pasty compound was too much for professors of special diet, to say nothing of exasperated surgeons.

Mrs. B—— showed the advantage of some previous training in a civil hospital in Massachusetts. Although of lower grade in refinement and education than most of the other nurses, she came in more intelligently to system and worked more efficiently under it. She was keen and wary. No cheat or malingerer could deceive her for a moment, "though there's a verse of scripter in the Bible," she said, "which tells us they'll deceive the very elect." Trim and neat as wax in person and work, her qualities soon told on her ward. Bed-quilts hung no more awry, and blankets were folded over straight and smooth. Crusts and parings, sloppy and cloudy cans and tumblers, crumpled newspapers and greasy cards disappeared from the little bedside tables. A glass as clear as light, with a flower in the season, or a little green spray, a smooth napkin, a freshly-washed feeding cup for the drink, a game-box, a book from the library, took their places. White curtains appeared in the windows, or green where the light needed softening to the sick eyes, prints on the walls, rocking chairs swinging with heroes, up and down the long board doors.

The cups and plates in the little ward-room glistened with cleanliness, and even the ugly stoves began to shine. "Loud conversational blasphemy" and the banging of doors went out of favor. One of the first things she "drew" from the "Sanitary"—why do so many honest people always use the qualificative instead of the noun?—was a lot of soft, light slippers for the men-nurses in the ward. She knew that the heavy creak of a boot is almost as intolerable to a patient as a "sympathizer" sitting on the edge of his bed. She knew what to ask for and what to do with it. No discharged, disabled man, or helpless, furloughed man ever left her ward, without a report of the case at the store-room and an outfit of comforts for the journey. No crowd of new patients came in, in ever so great confusion, without a quick, discriminating survey of their real and immediate wants and a similar report and supply. She possessed what many better educated women never attain—the ability to postpone the non-essential to the essential, and to distinguish clearly between them.

For more than three long years she served in her place without a furlough. A "little good black tea" was the only luxury, an occasional drive to the city to take a sick boy to the Commission's lodge the only holiday she wanted. She had quinsy, dysentery, and small-pox during her term of service,

and would hardly give up to either malady until threatened
with a sentinel at her door. From morning till night, and often through the cold, dragging hours till morning again, she
could stand unwearied, or sit within call in her little ward-
room, with her spectacles and her Bible, the only book she
ever opened, or her half-knitted sock or mitten. Alas! she was
scarcely ever "on terms" with the other nurses, and finally
boasted: "Me and them don't speak—none of us." This was
all very well till she was taken ill with small-pox, when Miss
H., who had curls, and feelings, and testimonial bracelets
from her patients, and a sentimental correspondence with
two or three discharged ones, and who for these amiable
weaknesses had suffered much from Mrs. B.'s criticisms, vol-
unteered to nurse her, and did it so faithfully and kindly that
Mrs. B. was melted and took her into superfluous forgive-
ness again. The only touch of sentiment I ever saw in Mrs.
B. was over some delicate china tea-cups, sent as a present
for the Superintendent's little mess. "They jest make one
dream of home," she said; she "wanted to cry over 'em."

The men-nurses fared scarcely better than the women at
her hands. "I don't take no orders from a *reduced corporal*!"
I inadvertently heard her answer one day to a mild suggestion of the wardmaster, whose military record she had been
looking up. But she was loyal to the powers in office. A mal-
content went to her room with some grievance concerning
the Surgeon in Charge. "I jest opened the door, and sot a
chair outside, and says I, will you please to take a seat in the
entry, sir? I don't want no one in my apartment who comes
a grumblin' to me with acquisitions against my superior officers! He's a father to me!"—she insisted, of the Surgeon
in Charge, who might be thirty years her junior—"he was always a father to me!"

The patients were very fond of her, as well they might be, for most of her quarrels and all her little plots and wiles were in their service and favor. She left the camp with the last of the sick in August of 1865, and after too short a rest, took a place again in a civil hospital in Massachusetts, where she died in a few months, broken down, no doubt, by her toils and vigils in the army.

Gifts to Soldiers

THE SANITARY COMMISSION GENEROUSLY FILLED all our requisitions. We did not very often call on them, believing that their supplies were more useful and more necessary on the field, or in the wake of the armies. Private friends, and others, friends though strangers, sent us many good things, part of the great mass of offerings taken no account of in any printed record of the gifts of the people to their soldiers. Barrels of flannel shirts and socks, gallons of choice wines and liquors, casks of homemade pickles very different from the coppery cucumber of the regulation; all these could be had unasked, or for the asking. "Why send the very old Port?" I heard some one remonstrate with Mr. W., of New York; "wouldn't the next best do ?" "No !" was the answer; "it is the best a man has that belongs to God—and the army." Among many such gifts came four boxes of London Port, which had this little story: the wine was sent by an English gentleman to Miss Nightingale, in the Crimea. It arrived just after the hospitals were broken up, and was returned with other parcels to the storehouse in London, where it was kept for a long time, and finally sold for some army charity. The purchaser sent it, for the sake of its history, to his friend, Mr. D., of New York, and so it came to us.

Here is a list of one lot of gifts among many from Mrs. ——: "Eighty-six flannel shirts, thirty-six pounds condensed milk, one cask sherry, one cask brandy, one cask porter, one box tea, ten gallons wine, twelve gallons sweetmeats, one cask pickled mangoes and tomatoes." Mr. A., of New York, sent forty-eight Boston rocking-chairs. Mr. Ware, of Boston, known and blessed in many camps and hospitals, sent a large and excellent box of games. Others sent saws, files, chisels, bits and bitstocks, knives and tools of all kinds for carving, drawing, paper and pencils, slates, puzzles, and books—good standard books, travels, biographies, and stories, not Reports of Societies for 1850, exploded Railroad Guides, and Child's First Readers with one leather cover torn off. Of these, indeed, we received altogether about a barrel full, and turned them in to be sold for the local fund. One hospital worker in bone, who learned to carve in relief, and to cut cameos with great delicacy, was, on his discharge from the army, furnished by his father, a New England farmer, with money to go abroad and study, and is now one of the honorable band of American sculptors in Italy.

No one can count up the value of these things, not only in the flannels for discharged, broken-down men, and woollen socks and mittens for convalescents going on guard in puddles of snow-water, but the distraction from pain in wounded men, the occupation and interest furnished to wretched, bored, half sick, half well, wholly demoralized men who huddle in a hopeless Ivan round the "red-hot sheet-iron stoves." I have seen a bagatelle table revolutionize the sulkiest "convalescent" ward in camp. In another a dull, despondent set of yesterday will be carrying on a brisk match from the spelling games today, and here is poor little F. with tremulous lips and bright eyes, being slowly dragged up with portwine and arrowroot, but ready to cry at a word—sitting up with the solitaire board, pegging away, all over smiles. Sergeant G. has opened an arithmetic class, and all the new slates are in request. A German is learning English on his, and writes me a little note on it at every visit, and the wardmaster, a bright, kind, and capable young fellow, has made excellent progress on his, in French, with the help of an old grammar, interpreted by the courtly and cheerful Charmoille, the Frenchman with the right arm gone.

But who shall count the comfort of the rocking-chairs? The little swinging motion seemed to work off something of the nervous irritation and pain. They were covered all over with a blanket and stuffed with pillows. The high back gave rest to the weary head, and a bit of board laid across the arms supported the wounded hand, or the book, or game-box. Clymer, of a Pennsylvania regiment, had one side of his face, with one eye torn away, and could not lie down at all. He said never an impatient word during the many weeks of his suffering, and when his rocking-chair came, "thought he didn't want anything more now, in the whole world."

The Book of Nonsense-verses,

> *There was a young lady in Spain*
> *Who couldn't go out in the rain,*
> *So she married a fella' who owned an umbrella,*
> *This artless young lady of Spain.*

> *There was an old lady in Sweden,*
> *Had she lived in the garden of Eden*
> *I really believe she'd have "called" upon Eve,*
> *This social old lady of Sweden, etc., etc.,*

had a great run, beginning with a long-faced "party" who "didn't care about it, well, really now, no, thank you," and "wondered what in the world people *could*"—etc., etc., and ended by shouting over it, and keeping it a great deal too long for the patience of the next man. "Brown, Jones, and Robinson" made the tour of the wards. B., of the 12th Maine, was particularly fond of them. B. was himself an amusing spectacle. He was really badly hurt, but drew such a fishy expression over his eye, and was so dismal for three minutes while you were asking about him, and made something between a grievance and a virtue of not having eaten his breakfast, and thought he could "worry down" an oyster or two, and took a pint of them on the spot, and then laughed all over—dangerously—at Robinson's dog being carried off by the Austrian *mouchard*, which he considered much the funniest thing in the book. Then there was a delightful black boy scuffling on a spring-board. The wards were continually sending up to borrow him, and offering to "whistle all day" for him to dance.

The Reading Room, with maps and pictures, files of papers, books, and stationery, was a great resource for those who were well enough to get to it, and an inducement to convalescents to leave the moody circle round the stoves in cold weather. Books circulated in the wards, and there were always half a dozen daily "Chronicles," and plenty of picture-papers for the men in bed. They enjoyed looking up their own skirmishes, and one couldn't delight them more than by affecting to recognize them; "There you are, over the parapet, waving the colors; I should know you in a minute!" There was a Doré-like sketch once in "Harper's Weekly," a troop-train of open cars rushing through the great Cumberland Cut. With the deep shadows and the little points and dashes of light touching a thousand confused and crossing bayonets, it was very effective. This was popular among the men; they would have it torn out and fastened against the barrack walls. The barrack walls showed the changes, too, in popular sentiment. One hero came down and another went up. First, there was Major Anderson. Then there was "Little Mac" in every size and color; Mac. leading the skirmishing fight in Western Virginia; Mac. at the head of his gorgeous staff; Mac. the husband and father; Mac. by the camp-fire, planning a (Peninsular) campaign; Mac., alas!—a comic one—going on board a gun-boat. Then he came down and, Burnside's wounded men coming in, Burnside went up. "Burnside's wounded" wouldn't suffer a word to be said against him. "He's every inch a gentleman and a soldier," one of the worst hurt said to me. Then came Hooker and Sherman and Sheridan and Grant, and Thomas with his placid fatherly face and slouch hat. Later, General Howard was a favorite. "*He's* a Christian," said Thomas Tully, of the New York 73d; "I've lived near enough to him to know him for a Christian, though I'm but a poor one myself." These appeared and disappeared on the barrack walls. Mr. Lincoln was always there; crowned with immortal green at Christmas, garlanded with field-flowers in May, draped with flags after victories and after defeats alike, till the dark day in April when the men came with streaming tears to beg a bit of crape to cover the face.

Soldiers were omnivorous readers, but many wanted a better order of books than novels and magazines. One of the frowziest of the "Inv'lids" was a devourer of everything Mr. Sumner wrote. Files of the "Scientific American" were in demand. The parsonage Cicero and the store-room Shakespeare went about the wards. Dickens was very popular. I think David Copperfield was the favorite story. Devotional books were cheerfully accepted and often faithfully read. Dr. Newman

Hall's "Come to Jesus" was always liked. Once only, this happened: a Defender came for a needle-book, and having unrolled and carefully examined it, took out a tract he found in it, and laid it gently on the table, as something he had no use for.

The voluntary gifts of friends were very useful in fitting out discharged, helpless men for the journey back to the poor home. These men had often lived up to their pay, sending it home, and, having no further claim on Government, would have been utterly destitute but for outside supplies. We felt that men returned to duty, too, if they had families dependent on them, had peculiar claims upon us. In December of 1863 there was a general clearing out and sending to the field of men who were determined to "go straight to Richmond, batter down the prison doors and let the prisoners out." These went away in fine spirits and good flannel shirts, with mittens to handle the cold fire-arms and do the camp work with. The mittens and gloves were capital for the hospital guard. There were some days when

> *"The wind was turned to bitter North*
> *That was so soft a South before,"*

when the sponge baths in the quarters were solid, and the sponges round and hard as paving stones, and every barrack window had to be curtained and stuffed with blankets. Looking out of the store-room window we could see the tall sentinel tramping by underneath, up and down, up and down. The "relief" comes occasionally, but it is rough work for men not over-strong. We look at his big red cold hands on the cold barrel, and wonder if it is conduct unbecoming a Superintendent and a lady to astonish him with a pair of mittens dropping out of the sky. He disappears round the corner; appears again; great paws redder and stiffer than before. We seize a pair from the shelf, and as the tramp, tramp, comes under the window, say sternly, "Guard!"; then drop and fall back. Sometimes one catches us, looks up, grins, bows, and says, "Oh! thank you!" Sometimes one doesn't, and stealthily looking out again we observe him tramp, tramping away from us, pulling on the mittens and spreading out his fingers fan-vise, and eying them with a satisfaction which seems to come out through his back.

The choice wines and liquors sent us were always useful. Government provision was ample and even munificent in many things. In others the supply was inadequate, or the quality poor, or the routine process of "drawing" a little too deliberate for emergencies. One might think, for instance, that in the ordinary wear and tear of hospital use and washing, old sheets, shirts, etc., might be had in quantities sufficient to supply all the rags needed. But not a garment or fragment of a garment can be used until it is regularly inspected and condemned, and all must be laid away in the linen-house till the inspecting officer comes down on his regular tour. The operations cannot wait for the Inspector, and we must have rags, bandages, etc., always ready in abundance.

Then what a resource were the Borden's cans of condensed milk, when now and then after heavy rains the country wagons could not ford the streams and the milkman never got in at all, or in the hot midsummer, when in spite of precautions the milk got in all sour. "Tarragona," the hospital substitute for port-wine, so useful in chronic diarrhoea cases, was wretched stuff. All the port-wine and all the good brandy we used came from private sources. The quarterly supplies of porter and sherry were entirely inadequate, even with the close watch of the Surgeon in Charge over the Dispensary; so were the supplies of corn-starch and farina, while of cocoa, barley, gelatine (requiring brandy, loaf-sugar, lemons, and much time and trouble to make it available in jelly which scarcely a Yankee would touch), and one or two other things, we had preposterous quantities. The gelatine we made useful chiefly in clear soup, but vast accumulations of barley over and above all possible broths and gruels, must have gone back at last upon the hands of the purveyor. That wretched man must have been buried in barley-cans at the end of the war.

It was a pleasant task to receive and give out these voluntary supplies. They were hampered with no regulations. All articles, except those for eating and drinking, were free as air to any who were in need, and the others were worked into the Special Diet system or reserved for the gravest cases. No rule was more necessary than the one forbidding the indiscriminate giving out of food and drink in the wards. No evasion of the rule was tolerated. Permission in proper cases was always easily got. I suppose the restriction bore sometimes hardly upon the "sympathizer;" perhaps occasionally on the patient; but think of the labor and anxious nursing and watching and preparing of delicate little messes for weeks, made naught by the visitor of an hour with his clandestine pie and sausage.

The Surgeon in Charge directed us to aim at strict impartiality in all our distributions. He was often annoyed by the visits of special agents who singled out men here and there and left the others disappointed. A nice basket of comforts pushes in at the door; air of expectancy and pleasure on every pale face; all the frowzy heads come up above the blankets. "Any Alaska soldiers here?" asks the cheery voice behind the basket. None, evidently, for all the pale faces and frowzy heads retire despondently under the blankets again. The Surgeon in Charge, present on one such occasion, said: "These are *United States* soldiers, my dear madam; pray treat them all alike as nearly as possible." He was usually at war with State Agents, a veritable "Ursa Major" we told him, with them, and evidently deprecated their existence. I believe he would, if he could, have blotted out all evidence of State organization.

Chaplain's Day

THE HOSPITAL ACKNOWLEDGED the blessing of a faithful Chaplain. Chaplain —— was ready at the lightest call, from sunrise to moonrise, and no night was too black or stormy to find him in the farthest corner of the camp bringing comfort to some soul in pain. The duties of the office were many and laborious. Besides the regular church services and writing of sermons, the singing and prayer meetings, Bible and Sunday school classes, funeral rites and constant ministrations to the sick and dying, there were the official Death and Burial Records to keep, the Moral Condition and History of the Hospital to write up for the Adjutant General; the Reading Room and Post Office to overlook, including the franking of soldiers' letters, sometimes thirteen hundred in a week, which would be only one apiece all round when the Hospital was full; "effects" to box and send home, and letters, perhaps twenty-five or thirty a day, to write to soldiers' families.

It was always touching to see the poor little bundles of "effects" going over to the parsonage; they were sometimes so very small; I remember one entry:—"Effects, one pair of shoes." And the shoes told such a story; tied together and

slung across the frayed and faded coat, the knapsack of var-
nished cloth all cracked and shabby,—the poor, broken, trodden down shoes, still stained and furrowed with the mud of so
many weary marches.

The letters to soldiers' families were no common, formal
statement of facts. They must be framed with care and con-
science. They carried precious things; the note-book leaf, the
hymn-card, the lock of hair, the plain gold ring; they carried
the last look backward of the parting soul: "Tell her I kissed
her picture and wished I had been a better man;" the little,
little gleam of light across the darkness of the invisible country: "He said some words at last that seemed like prayer." How
difficult such correspondence must often be, the Chaplain's
memoranda show:—

"Irrational since the day of his arrival.

Died in the ambulance at the door.

Does not want me to write home; has no message.

Says he 'does not get ahead with any religion.'

Wandering; one minute charging with his regiment and
the next with his mother at home.

Irrational; cried out, 'Mother, you are wanted,' and died.

Dying, said: 'The room is growing dark; are they putting
out the lights?' On the fly-leaf of his little diary was written: 'It
had been better for them not to have known the way of righ-
teousness.'

Could not understand; commended him to God's mercy;
could not hear."

Part of the Chaplain's burden was the hourly watch that
no chance of speaking for the better life should by any means
be missed. It was literally speaking—

"As never like to speak again,
And as a dying man to dying men"

It was patiently, painfully following the wandering soul through the perplexed mazes of fever, through the exaltation and horrible reaction of drugs and stimulants, through the craze of chloroform, to find the one sane and clear moment in which the name of the Lord Christ could be spoken.

Perhaps the saddest service was receiving soldiers' friends who came, often too late, or came to see "those who had tended him," or to hear "something more about him;"—always the cravings for "something more"—or to see "the place where he was lying." After H.'s death and burial, his mother came to see him. She was a gentle, sweet-faced old lady, with soft, pale cheeks and lovely gray hair. G. took her out to the graveyard, neat and quiet, where he lay. " Will you plant something on his grave ?" she asked. "Oh, yes," said G., "what would you like?" "I would like a white rose, dear." G. promised. "Would you kiss me, dear?" she said; and G. put her arms round her neck and kissed her soft, old cheek with tears. I heard a strange moaning in the lower hall one day, like the cry of some wounded creature, and going quickly down the staircase, found S.'s poor old mother, who had come alone from far out West, to see him, not knowing how rapidly he had failed. She had stopped at the Registry Office door, and, giving in the name, was thoughtlessly answered by the clerk in one word, "Dead." We got her up stairs and made her some tea, and she sat in a chair by the window, bending to and fro, and moaning softly all the afternoon, and saying not a word. Only the next day she was able to hear how good and faithful he had been as a nurse to his comrades, and how peaceful in his death.

The Chaplain was called on frequently to visit and bury the "contrabands" whose poor little huts hung upon the edges of the camp and were scattered over the fields all the way to the city. After the Second Bull Run battle large numbers of blacks gathered about the Hospital and were kindly treated, the men being employed in policing and the women as laundresses, all receiving Government rations. So great, however, was the temptation afforded by their abject ignorance that they were at one time nearly starved by an acting commissary steward, who was summarily dealt with by the Surgeon in Charge and made to give up his evil-gotten gains.

We always had a representative or two of the race at work in our quarters, delighted with wages and spending them chiefly in ribbons and copper trinkets in the town. Coming back after a furlough we find the last new Topsy of the establishment seated over against us at the bedroom wood-fire, a magnificent heap of blazing, crackling hickory logs, for we have begged to have the black cylinder with the roar, taken away. Topsy sits and gazes at us, and says from time to time:— "I know what your name is."—"Miss Leighton's got a baby."— "That there sack you've got on's pretty."—"I dunno as ever I see a breast-pin like that afore." She goes out, and presently returns, without knocking, actually to re-examine the bath-gloves, which fill her with astonishment, ostensibly because "she thought she heered me call," and, indicating with her shining elbow the letterpaper scattered on the table, she wants to know if I am writing to my "beau."

The huts about us, first homes of the wandering, sorrowful race, were strange patchwork; bits of shelter tents and blankets, ends of plank, barrel staves, logs and mud, but most of them were neatly whitewashed and with the likeness of a little, fenced garden behind, and near many and many, by the roadside, was a rough grave with a red-wood cross at its head. The huts and the gardens are gone, and the forlorn graves were trodden long ago into the fine, white dust of the Virginia highway.

In some of the Chaplain's cares nurses and Superintendent could share, as in writing of letters, etc., but the regular, methodical business was of necessity in his own hands, and was performed with utter devotion; "done to the Lord," heartily, and not to men, and done through circumstances of peculiar domestic anxiety and trial. The Chaplain's wife, herself an invalid, constantly visited and distributed comforts among the sick, and the parsonage children, carrying their oranges and their bunches of wild-flowers and their picture-papers, were a real "streak of sunshine" in the wards. It was pleasant to see the men fondle and talk to them, taking out their family pictures and comparing height and color: "He was a bit of a baby then—but he might now be just about as big as you." They were always pleased with little stories of the parsonage children's plays and talk; especially, I remember, with this one: Says little Johnnie, "Mamma, do the angels come down to us in the night? and"—with anxiety—"could I see one if I was to wake up quick?" "Oh, no, Nonnie," answers Eddie, the youngest, "we haven't got *the right kind of eyes.*"

Occasional help in preaching etc., was to be had from the city and the near forts, and from among the patients. The Superintendent sometimes found time to sing and read hymns in the wards, and was rewarded by the comments of such a slow boy as Bailey, who drawls: "Dear me, those hymns sound altogether different when you read 'em and when I read 'em myself." Reverend Mr. Dickerson, a detailed man, nurse in Ward E, sometimes held service. Captain A. assisted at the meetings. He was one of seven sons of a widow. Four brothers were in the field; one was at home disabled from wounds, and the youngest was an invalid. When the sixth son enlisted, the Captain followed the Chaplain's advice—as he would not be ready for heavy duty for six months—resigned and took up his theological studies again.

The Chaplain's labors had their compensations even at the moment. Many owed their acknowledgment of Eternal Truth to him. Many simple, heroic, Christian souls passed in his review, some going homeward, some heavenward, some back into the smoke of the fight, refreshed and renewed for either death or life. I quote, from memoranda made by him, a case or two among hundreds:

"J. B———. Sinking; knew no one, but recognized the name of Jesus and the tune, but not the words of the hymn we sang.

"W. J——— says: 'Write to my wife and tell her before this reaches her I shall be no more. I rest on Jesus and on Him alone. I see His blood. Tell her to a let my bosses lie here—*I* shall be in Heaven. I leave it her and the children in God's hands.

"W. O———. Chronic diarrhoea; emaciated to the last degree; says: 'Write to my father just how I am; don't conceal anything. I am giving you a great deal of trouble, but it strengthens me to have you here.' I asked, 'do you rest your hope of salvation on Christ?' He answered, 'I can do nothing else.'

"James T———. Had both feet amputated after wounds at the Second Bull Run fight. Dictated a letter to his mother; 'I am as comfortable as can be; doing first rate. God has supported me. My trust is in Him. I hope I shall have no discouraging word from you. It was you who taught me to trust in God. Before my legs were amputated I gave the Bible to ——— to send to you, not knowing how it would fare with me. I have the best of attention and food. Send me an account of how they got along with the hop-picking. I always enjoyed that season. Don't be scared. I consider myself worth a number of dead men yet.' This noble fellow got well and went home.

"Wm. McC——. Peacefully trusting in Christ. Expressed no anxiety to recover. As I was trying to repeat a psalm from memory, prompted me in the verses. Said: 'Write to my father and tell him I am very ill; that my whole trust is in Jesus.' Later he said: 'I want my family to know that religion has sustained and comforted me,' and stretching out his arms, cried, 'Jesus, I am coming,' and so died.

"Color-Sergeant D——. Shot through the right shoulder, had repeated hemorrhages. When sinking he said: 'Tell my mother I die in a good cause. I have carried the flag over the land of the brave and the free! Don't let those traitors run away with the country! Don't let them destroy the country! They should not as long as I could stand on my feet.' I said: 'Thanks be to God, who giveth us victory.' He answered: 'Yes; He conquers for me. I look to Christ for pardon.' He died that night."

The chapel services were always well attended, except now and then in times of great sickness and heavy work, or when the Hospital was, for the time, thinned out. The week-day prayer-meetings were greatly enjoyed by the men. The Chaplain was an Episcopalian, but instead of discouraging these assemblies as some Chaplains I have known, he quietly took possession of them, and so secured their being carried on with order and decorum. The prayers were like what only the prayers of men in the almost visible presence of death will be, if they pray at all. There were some men with special gifts of fervor. How H. prayed! We called him "the man who prayed so loud." I remember one night in particular; H. was to go back to the field next morning; it was the eve of some great movement or battle. He prayed for himself and his comrades; for the Surgeon in Charge; for the country. He took hold on Heaven. How the strong voice rang out again and again through the deep stillness of the camp: "I will not let Thee go, unless Thou bless them all! It may be the last time I can call on Thee, O Lord; I will not let Thee go!" A few days afterward word came back that H. was shot through the heart in a charge of the regiment. And how they sang! Was there ever anything like the singing of two or three hundred men in the shabby blue coats, on crutches, with heads bound up, and arms in slings, or empty dangling sleeves,—pale and wasted, lifting up their voices and pouring out their hearts upon the "Rest for the Weary," or "Homeward Bound," or "Shining Shore," or "Glory Hallelujah"? Once the night prayer-meeting was kept up till near tattoo, when an officer from one of the neighboring camps, who was present with a dozen of his men, got up, called out in a clear, ringing voice in the middle of the service: "Men of the —— Artillery, Forward—March!" and they clattered out. The officer was a devout helper in the meetings, but military rule was strongest in those days.

The extempore speech and prayer sometimes took odd turns. I was present at a meeting when a Defender rose and said he wished to confess to the brethren some particulars of a sinful life. There was once, in such a town, a godless youth— said he, and went on to paint his career; how at the age of twelve he smoked cigars and threw the Bible at his grandmother; at fourteen he played tenpins and went sailing on Sunday; at sixteen he ran away from home, etc., etc., and when we expected the usual conclusion, "and I who address you to-night, my friends, am that forsaken lad," he surprised us by clapping his hand on the shoulder of an innocent, blushing youth in front of him, one of the steadiest boys in camp, and shouting his climax, "Which his name is Asy Allen and here he sets!"

Holidays

W E KEPT ALL THE HOLIDAYS at the Hospital; feasts and fasts. The fasts were observed, not literally, but with chapel services. The feasts we were more exact about; fire-balls on Fourth of July, roast beef, pudding, and holly boughs at Christmas; but Thanksgiving was the best of all. There was the sermon on the blessings of the time; there was always enough to be thankful about, in the darkest days; and "Rally round the Flag, Boys," and "My Country 'tis of thee," and then the turkeys with their lovely gizzards chopped up in hot gravy, the mashed potatoes and onions stewed in milk, the cran-berry sauce, the pickles, the fruit-pies and puddings and iced-cakes trimmed with pink lightning, and the oyster supper in the evening, crowning all. It was wonderful how little harm came of these feasts. Almost unlimited permission to join in them was given by the surgeons, and I have reason to suspect that generous portions were smuggled in by their comrades to the water-gruel patients; but there seemed to be a charm in the home holiday strong enough to divert the pie-crust and the stuffing from their natural consequences.

Poor Sergeant S—— didn't think he cared about any Thanksgiving. What was Thanksgiving to him? Now if he were at home and could have it all quiet and nice with his friends,—but the mess-hall and the crowd and the quantities of things and the smell and the noise,—and then he didn't believe there would be a single bit of celery, or even cranberry sauce. Poor Sergeant S. had come to the field full of the right zeal and spirit at first, giving up a salary of a thousand dollars for thirteen dollars a month "and the country," but he was utterly broken down with over-marching, exposure, and long sickness. Wouldn't he like to have his dinner brought in to him? "No. He didn't want any dinner. What had he to do with Thanksgiving?"

In the great wings of the central building were many little rooms set apart for patients. To very ill, or nervous and sensitive men their quiet and cheeriness were a great blessing. Each room had one or two white beds for patients and one for an attendant, each its little open fireplace and crackling wood-fire, and high, wide window letting in the sweet sunshine and the sight of the sailing clouds, the pleasant fields, the far-off, gleaming river. Sergeant S. had one of these rooms. At dinner time he was enticed for a moment into one next door, and when he came back, his little table was set out for dinner with a white cloth, a fresh damask napkin folded over the block of bread, a change of hot china plates, the Superintendent's silver fork and spoon, a covered dish with the turkey, another with vegetables, a little bowl of cranberry sauce and a crisp spray of celery in a tall flowerglass. The poor Sergeant melted and came to again, forgot his vapors and ate every crumb of his little feast. I think he got better from that day.

Sometimes, when the Hospital was thin, we took a holiday ourselves, and walked out into the sweet brown waste beyond the camp to see how the seasons got on.

All seasons were delightful here, even the hot midsummer "when the hay was down;" when walking was impossible before dusk and impracticable after it; when the town and the river lay invisible in pure heat; even then, though the store-room thermometer rarely got below 86° and stood from 96° to 101° for many days together,—little breezes were always blowing about the papers on the table, and on the tower top in the rare evenings when we found time to go up, it was another country. From the tower top we watched the swallows in broad flights, wheel and scatter and close again and drop by twos and threes and handfuls into the wide chimneys. There was one swallow, a gay young bachelor swallow, who came home with the family, but when all was quiet popped his head out of the chimney again, looked about him, hopped up on the top ledge, fluttered a little and was off like an arrow. We caught him at it two or three times. "He had only come back for his latch-key; he meant to make a night of it," said the Surgeon in Charge.

First after our Hospital life began, came the long and late Indian summer when the river was a line of smoky blue and the dome hung a great white bubble in a purple sky. Then came the light pure snow-falls of January and the wonderful February ice-storms turning everything to glass and diamond, as if a fairy godmother had touched the whole world with her wand; and then more beautiful, if possible, the unlocking of the spell;—all about the place such a rattling and clashing, sliding of the roofs, loosening from spouts and rails and cornices, klinketing against the window-ledges, showering in rains of jewels with every light wind in the trees;—all the fairy frostwork going to pieces; and through the clinging white mist of the soft morning; a sudden splendor of clear sunshine flashing over all. Then came wild March days with flying clouds and ink-black streaks and spots of shadow on the river and the distant shores; the white line of the city coming out with startling distinctness in every momentary gleam.

The March days were sometimes wild indeed. One fearful wind-storm overtook us. Looking out of the store-room window in the morning I saw the first sign of its coming in a sudden swirl of light leaves into the air. Then a huge white cloud came all at once across the levels from the city, with the scream of a fiend behind it. The dome was just visible, a lead-colored ball through the white dust-storm. Then all the red-brown leaves from all the bushes in the fields were in the sky at once, pouring in over the open top of the window, even driving down the chimney. Then John put his head in at the door, with the grin of one who announces a calamity, and said, "Ward A and Ward B has went and Ward G is a-going." I ran to the window, and in an instant, with a powdery crash, over went Ward G all its length on its side. A crowd of men carrying others came out at its upper end, then a puff of smoke from the roof. The stoves were upset.

For a moment I was very anxious, expecting to see the whole tar-roofed range one sheet of wind and flame. There was a rush of the "Fire Brigade" for the buckets, standing, always filled, with the axes and ladders, on the first landing of the central building. I tried to get out at the front door. The wind stood up against me like an iron wall. There was nothing to do but to collect and fill the store-room cans and buckets and set them out ready. Happily a great burst of rain came with the next stroke of the gale, and the fire was soon got under. All the patients were taken out unharmed, except by the shock and a scratch or two, and transferred to other wards. The barracks were so utterly wrecked that repairs were impossible, and in their places, by and by, rose beautiful, airy, fresh tent-wards in which it was almost a pleasure to be ill.

By middle-March the trees in the grove began to look alive. A sort of green mist softened the distance. From the store-room window spring could be plainly seen; the sweet, early, half-Southern spring, with its inexpressible charm. Getting shrubs and trees in mass and fields aslant in wide spaces gives the tender greens and yellows a chance to show. The air is full of vague, earthy sweetness. One little bird begins to sing in a leafless tree near the store-room window, and sings all day the same little song; sings persistently, never heeding spiteful dashes of wind and rain; sings *dacapo* and *dacapo*.

Patches of snow lie by the road-side and in the fields; a fair, stiff crust,—like the rebellion we say, looking hard and defiant till you set your foot on it. Crocuses push up among the weeds in the old garden-place, and we think it must be time to go out and look for trailing arbutus. Over the sweet brown waste, beyond the earthworks, half way down the first ravine, we find it. Light mats of snow lie over it; snow-mats shrunken away at the edges, pierced by a hundred grass-blades. Under the red-oak shrubs, under the dry, rustling leaves, under the yellow fern, we find it, bed after bed of it; just not in blossom; buds all streaked with white and pink.

A week afterwards, after a day or two of soft rains, we go again,—and all the slopes of the ravine are fairy-land with thousands of downy pink and white blossoms, all fragrant with the blessed odors of the woods. We take them up in handfuls and baskets full, and by the strong fibres in the moss-beds as they grow, and the store-room and wards are filled with their sweetness for days.

A little later other spring flowers came; liverwort, starflowers, anemones, low blossoming shrubs and millions of violets. Everywhere the ground was only one great tufted mat, yellow, white and blue; along the roadside, creeping up to the very edges of the earthworks; following round in fairy-rings the circles where the old Sibley tents stood last year; broad-sown in the wide, empty fields—millions on millions of wild flowers. They were a constant delight to us all. The men dug them up and planted them in short-lived gardens by the barracks, the children brought them in tin-cups full and aprons full, and every ward was gay with garlands and bunches of them.

This freedom of the fields now and then, with the glimpses of the lovely changing seasons, was a wonderful rest and refreshment after the anxiety and sadness of the wards and the endless routine of the store-room. These were our sweet and priceless holidays.

One evening near the May of 1864 the Surgeon in Charge came to the door and asked if we would like to see the watch-fires of an army. There were "a thousand fires," he said, "between Xanthus and the ships, and fifty warriors to each, and the horses were munching their barley-heaps and waiting for the morning." From the tower top we saw the camps lying, twinkling, a field of fire-flies toward the North; big lights, little lights, and a sort of luminous mist where the lights all ran together. The next morning we went through the camps, and the hundreds of shelter-tents, rows of glittering brass guns, pickets of horses, red blankets, blue uniforms—half a dozen black regiments drilling, among them—all grouped and scattered over the green fields by the river, made a gay and charming picture.

Again, the next morning, seeing a line of dust moving towards us through the grove, we knew it was a marching column and must be Burnside's men, so we went to the bottom of the field and waited on the grass to see them go by. They looked so well, so cheery. It was a delight, accustomed as we were to the gaunt faces in the wards, to see so many healthy-looking men. They marched at ease, laughing, singing, calling out now and then, "Good-bye, ladies! Good-bye!" One tall fellow dipped his tin cup in a little spring by the roadside and drank our healths in passing. "*Ave Caesar*," said the Surgeon in Charge; "*Morituri te salutant.*" The sod was thick with violets, and bunches of them were stuck in many caps and coats. A soldier took the cluster from his cap-band and gave it to me. G. unfastened a little gilded horseshoe from her chain and tied it, by the blue ribbon, in his coat. He lifted his cap; "This will keep me safe in the next battle; I did not expect such good luck in Virginia." One company was singing in parts,

"Rally round the Flag, boys,
Rally *once again!*"

A New Hampshire regiment, a New York and a Pennsylvania regiment looked very finely; toughened through and through, red-brown faces, dusty, blonde hair and white teeth; looked as if no camp-sickness could get hold of them. "Didn't know where they were going; only were going after Jeff. and meant to give it to him when they got him." So they passed, marching and singing, the bayonets disappearing at last southward in the spring sunshine, in the dust of the Leesburg pike.

In the wake of the column crept a shabby, stealthy country wagon with a dirty canvas cover, conducted by two dun-colored natives of the class called "loyal residents of the neighborhood." Armed with his rank and his suspicions, the Surgeon in Charge ordered a halt and found the wagon packed full of blue overcoats thrown away on the warm, dusty march. He took possession of course, and turned the property over to the nearest quartermaster.

One day when the Great War was drawing to a close, we heard that the troop-ship Atlantic was at the wharf below, taking on a part of Schofield's Army Corps to reinforce General Sherman, and drove down to the town to see the embarkation. The ship was not quite ready, and the wharf and the near streets were blue with uniforms. One Indiana and two Illinois regiments were to go on board. We went up into the great ship for a moment and looked down on the wharf. It was heaped with boxes, bales, barrels, knapsacks, little leather trunks, camp-chairs, and all the indiscriminate "plunder" of the regiments. Muskets were stacked all up and down the streets running from the wharf, and the men were "house-keeping" on the curb-stones. Commissaries were breaking open barrels and boxes and giving out rations; fifty little camp-fires made of the staves and boards were smoking away, and fifty coffee-pots and tin cups simmering over them. An officer with a charming face and manner came up and spoke to the Surgeon in Charge. "Rough work this and hard fare"— pointing to the biscuit the men were carrying off in their blankets; "but I've seen more than one day when we were after Hood when I would leave given five dollars for one of those hard tacks, aye and for half a one." The men, he said, were in the finest spirits with the prospect of going to Sherman. They were a noble-looking set. "Where are you going ?" we asked one and another. "Ah! to Sherman! *He's* the soldier!" "May I warm my hands at your fire?" I asked one group. It was early February and very cold. "That you may," said two or three at once, jumping up, though they had nothing better than the curb-stone to offer me as a seat—"That you may, only"—

looking at me—"you mustn't mind having the smoke in your eyes." But I don't think it was the smoke. They told me they left Thomas on the 15th of January at Clifton and expected to enjoy the voyage and seeing "new countries" very much.

We had just heard of Mr. Lincoln's journey to Fort Monroe to meet the rebel commissioners, but the result was not yet known. "If it's a patched-up peace the soldiers won't see it," said one of the group about the fire, and another: "I guess old Abe will come out about right. He generally suits *me* whatever he does."

"Do you lose your men," we asked our unknown officer, "when they scatter in a town like this ?" "Oh, no," he said; "in all our marches I have only lost, once four, once six men, and they joined us at the next halt. Our regiment never lost a man in *that* way."

In the Store–Room

THE STORE-ROOM FIRE CRACKLES AND SPARKLES, catching at the little crisp scrolls of bark on the edges of the birch logs and sending light, flashing flames up the chimney. The store-room window is open; it is almost always open all the year round. They are raising the flag. It stops at the half-mast this morning and a voice under the window says: "Robinson got his discharge last night." Other distant flags here and there, little bits of light and color, toss in the soft wind. A long drawn strain of far-off band-music comes in, cut sharply across by the kling! kling! of the office orderly-bell. This frequent stroke of the office bell gives a wonderful sense of comfort and security. The Chief Officer is at his post; when is he not at his post? and all the machinery is in swift and even motion.

A grievance or two are lying in wait for me at the door. Sullivan holds a can of butter in silent protest under my nose, and seeing plainly my acquiescence in his own views, says: "I wouldn't cheat the slush fund of that there butter, ma'am, no how." It is Steward Blank's last "bargain." By and by I hold a little conversation with Steward Blank on the subject of butter, but he soon diverts it to the religious interests of the

Hospital and what "we officers" owe the men in the way of example. But the caduceus even when worn across the shoulder, as Steward Blank wears it, to give an air of rank, inspires me with very little respect.

> I know a Steward fair to see,
> Trust him not!

"No boiled eggs in Ward D for breakfast." Investigation shows that the eggs of Ward D, a rare accident, were set on the wrong tray and quietly partaken of by the ward next above without any attempt to right the blunder. Sullivan anxiously offers to avenge on E, D's injury, but it is not too late to send a fresh supply, and it is perhaps asking too much of the Defenders that when fortune places unexpected eggs before them, they should reject the gift.

Ben, the cheerful and profane butcher—why are we called on to tolerate so much "language" in the butcher?—comes to assure me that something is the matter with the "specific levity" of the mutton and poultry, "for things weighs entirely different here and in town," and, reminding me that there is a "special" for broiled chicken for one, wants to know "if he shall kill half a chicken."

Little Wood, carpenter, undertaker, and unreserved veteran, is putting a new lock on the store-room door. "It is well known, ma'am," say certain of my ward friends, "that more than one key in this institution unlocks your door." Wood is weazened and elderly, small and sharp, with a keen lookout for objects connected with his profession, and eager to entertain us with professional anecdotes. It is a great trial to him to see so much punch making going on in the store-room "and he not in it." "A good many pretty bad off in the 'ospital," he says:—"There'll be *one* in Ward L, to-night, and *one* in K, or me name's not Wood;"—begins to wheeze—"I'm pretty bad

meself !"—appeal to my sympathy;—"thought I should have
to give up me job altogether;"—appeal to my interest.—"I'm
sorry you don't feel well;" wheezes rise into groans accompanied by appealing glances at the rows of punch bottles waiting for Ward D. It is enough to melt a heart of stone. I don't
give in. I know it will be the costly first step; that Wood will be
taken ill on the premises every day thereafter; I urge peppermint tea upon him and settle our relations on the whiskey
question forever.

The Surgeon in Charge is making rounds this morning.
The kling! kling! ceases for awhile, and Templeton, best of
men-nurses, arrives and says; breathless with haste and importance: "Some of the good brandy, please'm, and a lot of soft
handkerchiefs—Surgeon in Charge—operation in G."

The Surgeon in Charge made a midnight round last night,
the nurses say, to see that all was well.

We are proud when special orders signed by him come in,
and fill them with the very best in store. He often sends us a
word or two from his notes, to help us, he says, to cook with
intelligence.

Number 822 had swallowed nothing for a week. It was good
to get such a bulletin as this:—"Finding 822 pulseless, a sharp
knife down his throat reached and evacuated the abscess. He
is taking nourishment.

Have just trephined N. and W. As soon as I raised the bone
both showed consciousness and spoke. Make some weak,
sloppy gruel for them.

Am going to M. to tie the gluteal artery and to remove a
ball behind the eye. Have a quart of wine-whey and a quart of
egg-nog ready.

Saw H. Made an opening in the thigh and introduced a
drainage tube. He will do well. Eggs and brandy, as much as

he will take.

D. P.'s hand can be saved. Shall see that it is done. 'The man with the head' in G is doing finely.

L. is a humbug. I will restore him to the bosom of his family.

Number 403. Shot through the neck. Send only the thinnest liquids, wine-whey, liquor of oysters, etc., till further notice.

Send Keith one raw egg beaten in a teaspoonful of brandy every hour.

Send James C. twenty-four ounces of port-wine for twenty-four hours. Also, boiled milk and one soft or raw egg every two hours.

Send Weitman a quart of milk-punch made with brandy, and some crackers and dried beef in place of his rations; he goes home discharged. Send him also a pair of large leather slippers.

Went to Ward G to amputate C.'s right arm. I explained why I think it necessary to the poor fellow, who acquiesced quietly but sadly. After he was etherized, put my finger into the wound, saw a chance and excised the elbow. He will do well. Eggs and brandy."

The Surgeon in Charge believed in food as a curative agent. He ordered it in large quantities for men who had suffered severe operations; and our experience certainly justified his theories, for these men got well, went home, had the small-pox, married their sweethearts, set up shops and wrote back for all our photographs to hang up in them. Vandenhoff, Sawyer, Tyler, McClain, Ripley, Brown, Gregg; a host of names suggest themselves. All these took large quantities of beef-essence, and brandy and eggs to the extent of one half-pint tumbler full every two hours.

Sergeant G., exsection of shoulder, Dec. 25th, 1863, took oyster soup, chicken soup, eggs at every meal prepared in different ways, besides forty-eight ounces of egg-nog and two to three bottles of porter every day for several weeks. He then came under the ordinary special diet table and took roast beef, vegetables and pudding with one or two pints of milk-punch every day. Early in March he was able to travel and was discharged and went to Philadelphia, where he was promised a good place as watchman. The Sergeant enjoyed all his meals and showed no failure and certainly no delicacy of appetite, as he had an immense craving for an article, furnished, he declared, in perfection only by the Philadelphia markets, the intestines of a hog compounded with spices. To gratify him inquiries were made, but this savory dish could not be obtained.

Lafayette R——, Tenth Vermont Vols., exsection of elbow, was able to eat almost immediately after the operation, and consumed an extraordinary amount of food. He began with beef-tea and egg-nog, taking, in the first twenty-fours after the operation, twenty-four eggs beaten in twenty-four ounces of brandy with the usual proportion of milk, and a table spoonful of the strongest essence of beef every two hours. This was prepared by semi-broiling the beef, cutting it into dice and expressing the juice with lemon-squeezers. I gave him in this way, in one day, the juice of thirteen pounds of lean beef besides his other food. In three days he began to take porter, decreasing the quantity of brandy and eggs and increasing the porter till he took seven pint-bottles a day, besides three meals of the ordinary special diet, such as beef-steak, large quantities of potatoes mashed with milk and butter, stewed oysters, scrambled eggs, chicken, custards, etc. He lay in his bed and fed, serenely, "without haste, without rest."

His capacity astonished all beholders. When able to travel he was transferred to Vermont. A letter from him four months afterwards, says: " My arm gains strength rapidly, and I think it will be nearly as good as the other. I am in charge of the Dispensary and my general health is perfectly good."

McC., exsection of the shoulder, began to take oyster broth and milk-punch soon after the operation, and consumed, regularly, large quantities of food. He took steak, baked potatoes and milk toast for breakfast; roast beef, vegetables, and custard for dinner; a bowl of oysters between meals, and egg-nog, ale or porter every two or three hours. He improved rapidly, was contented and merry, and said he wanted nothing but a copy of "Rasselas to see if the Happy Valley was anything like —— Hospital." His recovery was a little hindered by the arrival of an elderly relative with a large box of doughnuts, sausage and pound-cake with the heavy streak, in which the patient privately indulged as long as they lasted. He travelled comfortably to Michigan in seven weeks after the operation, and soon after his arrival was taken ill with small-pox which was prevalent in his town, but afterwards wrote expressing his gratitude to the Surgeon in Charge and saying he "had no pain, that the arm gained strength very fast, and that he could use it and the hand quite well."

Walker, the store-room orderly, was a valuable assistant and faithful friend. He ran about untiring, all day, carrying puddings and pickles and shirts and sherry bitters to the men. If he saw any one he fancied very ill or overlooked, he was sure to bring the story with kind eyes full of sympathy. They all knew Walker's shining face—he was a fresh young fellow— and often sent their little messages by him. "There's a man in M. says he's awful empty and wishes he could have something to fill him up. Couldn't I take him a corn-starch pudding?"—"I wish Henry in Ward K could have a woollen shirt. He won't ask for it, and those two men-nurses are so slow they're as good as dead." His kindheartedness overran the bounds of camp. "There's a man out there in the fields"—a loyal Virginian so called—"sick in a hovel with nothing to eat." So we get a chicken from the mess and let him have the pleasure of taking it out and showing the wretched family how to make it into broth, a process of which they seem to have no idea, and he trudges away with it merrily a mile or two in the mud.

The business of looking over the special returns and written requests to classify them for filling, reveals abysses of evil spelling. "Lemons and sugar for 3 patience."—"Number 35 has one egg each meel."—"Beaf tea and a bole of gruel."—"Rags for poletasses."—"Milk porage for two."—I find with concern that evil spelling hardly seems to me the atrocity it seemed two years ago. Colonel W., of the Judge Advocate General's Department, declares to me: "What we really need, as a people, is punctuation; if we could only *mind our stops* all might yet be well." I am astonished to find in the Land of the Spelling-Book such defiance of its commonest laws.

I am astonished, too, to find so much helplessness in the use of the ordinary means of communicating ideas. A sheet of white paper, ghost-like, seemed to frighten and confuse, and hindered instead of facilitating business. From the letters received from inquiring friends, down to the smallest blank employed in hospital, where every device was used to get at just the information needed, everything seemed sometimes a hopeless "muddle." The Chief Officer soothed his irritation by the printing of a large placard behind which he took refuge, refusing to notice "mutilated scraps," but for the Superintendent there was no such relief.

Assistant Cook John comes in and presents four "specials" for dinner to-day and wants to know "whatever shall he do for chicken and steak and mutton and custard to be ready, at twelve and it's now half past twelve and they're always a doin' it a sending in fresh orders after dinner when the surgeon don't get round early and all the things drawed this morning and I to leave the pots a bilin' and come up to you."—I give him instructions, and requisitions on the commissary steward which calm his troubled soul.

After dinner hosts of visitors from the wards pour in, pale, limping and frowzy, mud-stained and ragged. They are late arrivals and many arm-slings are in demand. "I was a tailor; no more work for me now," says C., with two-thirds of his right hand shot away. People grumble because there's "no more play for me now;" how desolate the life must be in which is left neither work nor play. Here are scarves which must eke out the slings. On one is a writing: "Twice around the neck and once across the chest of the Union soldier, and the Young Ladies' Society of South Socrates, Maine, will be much pleased with a line from the recipient." I unroll several slings with the S. C. mark, made of an old-fashioned yellow-flowered fabric like faded bed-curtains. Pinned on the parcel is a slip of paper on which is written in a tremulous hand: "This material was so strong I thought the color would be no matter. It was all I had. I am old and poor and cannot do much." The unknown maker may be sure that more than one man read her words with tears in his brave eyes.

At last the arm-slings are all gone but two. One is a white silk scarf, a funeral scarf worn long ago at Doctor Kane's funeral. I fasten it over a tall man's shoulder and tell him what it is. He is delighted, for he has read the story of the strange North regions which are neither land nor sea and "Kane was always a hero of his." Now there is only one left, and the last soldier, the blonde big Sharpshooter from Michigan, positively refuses to take it.—"Somebody will certainly come along this afternoon who wants it more than I do." I offered a pair of loose slippers in the ward to-day to a man taking his first steps out of doors.—"Give 'em to that fellow over there," he insisted,—"he needs 'em a heap more than I." A tall skeleton comes in to see if he can get an orange for a sick man who cannot come for it. "But don't you want anything for yourself?"—"Oh no, I'm ever so much better off than he is; I'd rather take something for him." *Thy necessity is greater than mine.*

Two men in tattered clothes hobble in. The clatter of their crutches is irresistible. Am I "the Sanitary?" they ask, so I produce my reddest flannels, and they run like a flaming torch through all the camp. Twenty more come at once for red flannel shirts; blue will not answer; red is the color that suits their constitutions. I fall an easy prey. I give them out as far as they go, to the lamest and most ragged. Better that ten unrighteous should have two shirts apiece than the one model of the virtues go shivering.

A Zouave looking seven feet high wants many things. I give him socks; I give him handkerchiefs; I give him letter paper; I give him tobacco; I give him everything he asks for; he is so big. They tell me about their journey into Fredericksburg; a march of horrors. It is always the same story; marching and halting and marching, over frightful roads with endless delays; the "lighter cases," shattered arms, etc., having to walk; nothing to eat or drink; no care, no shelter;—And there were fellows left in the swamp who couldn't move;" one says: "I don't believe they were ever found."

Patient from Ward D calls to say he would like the ladies to join the Hospital Temperance Union; meeting for organization to-night; speeches and resolutions; hopes all will be present; feels as if he had been raised up as an instrument.

Ward surgeon calls to say that several ladies of his acquaintance are coming down to visit the forts and camps, could we supply them with bedding? Explain to the kind-hearted old Doctor, whom I should be very glad to oblige, that the only pillows, etc., under our control are sent for the exclusive use of the sick in hospital.

Another patient from the wards comes with a plea for tobacco. We hope he will not get small-pox, which has appeared in his ward.—"Oh no !"—he says,—"My family physician, old Doctor Stiles, told me I'd never ketch anything, I chewed too much tobacco for that." "But"—sententiously—"that was encouraging a bad habit." "Well"—jocosely—glancing at the big box just opened,—"It is a bad habit, but I'm too old to leave it off, and anyhow I shan't ketch the small-pox, for it only goes about in cold weather; my family physician, old Doctor Stiles, says so."

A nurse calls to say that the men *will* steal the towels. Show her that towels are a sacred trust of the Government, and if any towels are to be stolen she must direct the men to steal ours and not hospital property.

Poor Mason sends a message for pie. He wants pie on the brink of eternity. He seems turning all animal just before he turns all spirit. The surgeon says nothing will make any difference so I send him an apple turnover. The New Englanders, especially, never wavered in their love of "pie." The sick clamored for it and ward surgeons prescribed it. They seemed to consider it a light and pleasant article of diet, much to the disgust of the Surgeon in Charge, who issued more than one edict against it.

Three Defenders call to say that they have seen some needles and thread that "Jones got here," and would like to have some too. Three more Defenders who had seen the gentlemen who had seen the needles and thread that "Jones got here," would like more of the same sort, and the chairman of the delegation performs a bow and says "you're welcome, ma'am," meaning "thank you."

A jolly Blue-boy announces himself as the "near wheel horse of the diet car" and wants some dominoes and promises not to play on the top of the car on the out journeys. He says: "Mr. French, 'the off horse,' is on a pass to the city to hear the debates."

The Surgeon in Charge gave passes in large numbers to the men to hear the speeches and see the public buildings. He said many soldiers were from Western towns and might never have another chance. I do not remember any case in which this kindness was abused. These visits were well talked over and public questions well fought over in the wards. The Emancipation Proclamation, and the Message of December, 1863, with its plan of amnesty and reconstruction, ending with the words: "We do honorably recognize the gallant men, from commander to sentinel, to whom more than to others the world must stand indebted for the home of Freedom disenthralled," etc., etc., were folded down in the "Morning Chronicle" and handed approvingly from bed to bed. The Soldiers' Voting bill, the Bounty, Back Pay and Appropriation bills, the Peace plans and the Constitutional Amendment to abolish slavery, were thoroughly and intelligently discussed. Some of our men were present at all the great speeches of those days and many of them joined in the hurrahs and the "Glory Hallelujahs" of the 31st of January, 1865, when the Amendment was carried in the House.

At the re-inauguration every man who was well enough went over, the Surgeon in Charge, then and always, ordering that the enlisted men should have the first claim in the ambulances.

Looking out of the window in a break in the stream of visits, I see a poor, shabby, country wagon stopping at the main entrance and a pale woman putting her head out, covering and uncovering her face, searching the windows of the Hospital, looking for something she is afraid to see. Going down quickly in fear lest it should be Mrs. Robinson, whose husband died last night, I meet the man helping the woman gently in. "Mrs. Bendon, ma'am, my wife ;" and she,—"*Is* my son alive?" "Oh yes! alive and better."

The Surgeon in Charge, who has been interested in this ease, beckons me from the office and says he will go with me and see Robert. He stands by him and speaks to him about a furlough and going home, or having his friends come to see him; how would he like that?—"Oh, I know!" whispers Robert with the color all up in his forehead. "They've come; they're here now; I knew the moment you came in." So the father and mother sit by him, one on each side, happy to find him alive, happy to find a hospital a comfortable place; "they wouldn't have believed it; they have heard such stories!"

Robert has a sunny little room in the south Wing, with his rocking-chair and wood-fire and pictures and geranium-plant. "The mother would never have believed it," says the father; "I wouldn't have brought her, only I was afraid she would go crazy if Robert were to die. Two other mothers in our place in Ohio have lost their minds when their boys died, away in the army and they never saw them." They left the other children at home, and, helped by all the little settlement about them, set off on their long journey. "How did you get means for it?"

"Oh, the neighbors were very kind when they heard about it, and they came in, one after another, and brought us little packages of food, and we sold our horse; the neighbors got together and bought it at a good price."

And sitting by Robert's fire they told the simple little story, one among *so* many; the story of the quiet little settlement, so quiet, now that the boys were gone to the war; the anxious hearts, the daily toiling for the children left, while father's and mother's thoughts were following the weary, patient army; the gloom, when for two households in the very small village only the story of a soldier's grave was left; the horror, when insanity covered the grief of two mothers. All this they told, in their simple way, never seeing how pathetic it was, and how paltry it made much that the rest of us call sacrifice.

In a few days Robert was better able to travel, and, furnished with all the comforts of the Sanitary Commission, they set out on their slow journey to the log cabin and the carpenter's bench,—to privation sometimes, I am afraid, but to the home, where the neighbors were looking for them, and the children had the warmest nook by the fire saved for Robert; home, where he lived tranquil and happy till the spring passed, and the summer brought him Heaven.

Now, four or five discharged men come in to say "Good-bye" and get little comforts for the morning journey.

Bates,—left hand amputated.

Adams,—hip crushed at Chancellorsville.

Couch,—chronic diarrhoea.

Clark,—right arm amputated.

Christian Spann,—an amiable patient German from Michigan, fracture of both jaws and end of tongue taken off.

C. N.,—was buried alive in the explosion of the mine at Petersburg and has lost hearing, speech and almost all sensation. He has a piteous expression of face and makes signs as best he can, of gratitude for even a look of sympathy.

J. C.,—ophthalmia; losing the sight of both eyes, having several children at home depending on the work that he will never do again.

A.,—on crutches, is "really ashamed to ask for anything, but has lost his wife since he came out, and must save and look out for the children; three of 'em; oldest is thirteen, and trying the best she can to keep the little place together till he can get home to her."

A Connecticut man from Ward I comes in, he says, "for a little talk, if I don't mind." He is a typhoid convalescent and begins the "little talk" by asking if I have ever had a fever. "Yes," I answer; "I had a fever when I was in Rome." He smiles; something in the phrase "reminds him of Cassius." "In Rome?"—he says,—"You have been in Italy?" "Yes." "And have seen the antiquities and the Florence galleries and Raphael's frescoes and Michael Angelo's Last Judgment, and Pompeii and Vesuvius?"—all in a breath—"Oh! you have seen all these?" I admit the fact. "How happy I should be if I thought I should ever see what I long so much for." I suggest the theory that every intense, legitimate desire is prophetic of its own fulfilment, not necessarily here, but in another world if we fulfil the conditions of entering it. "I accept the theory"—he rejoins, kindling,—"but what then must we think of the future of such men as Chesterfield, for instance, who have expended themselves within the limits of life and time?"

The sun goes down beyond the sweet, brown waste with a touch of fire, here and there, on shining objects in the far-off town. The outline of the finished figure of Liberty—finished at last—grows dark against the reddening sky. The early evening is so fresh, so still. At dusk the men come under the window and sing, in parts, "Beautiful Star" and "Do they think of me at Home," and Walker goes down with hands full of tobacco and the assurance that they *do*. I don't think they sing "Glory Hallelujah" quite so much now, as "When this cruel War is over."

The store-room fire is a heap of glowing brands, just not fallen into glowing coals. The window is always open. How the whippoorwills cry! Bird-ghosts, invisible by day, haunting the grove and calling to each other out of the heart of it, in clear, shrill notes, sometimes faster and faster, as if one were trying to outcry his fellow; *whip-poor-will! whippoor-will! whip-poorwill! whippo'will! w'pw'll!* then a little silence, then a solitary cry and answer, and the airy duel over again.

Fragments of bugle-music from the distant forts float in on little puffs of wind. The Hospital bugle takes up the golden call and seems to say, sweet and slow,

> *"Hence, away;—all is well;*
> *One—aloof—stand—sentinel."*

In the Wards

B ESIDES THE DAILY DETECTIVE ROUNDS, much of the time that could be saved from the store-room was spent in the wards. Seeing the men constantly, learning their fancies and home habits, noticing the changes in their condition from day to day, gave real assistance in the special business of feeding them; and talking with them, writing for them, helping them invent occupations and amusements, hearing their "views" on public questions and witnessing always their wonderful courage and cheerfulness, were never-failing sources of refreshment and pleasure. The capacity of the Hospital was twelve hundred; but a current of men was always flowing in and flowing out, making the labor much heavier than any steady pull would be. Sometimes only a few came and went. Sometimes hundreds arrived or were swept off in a day. On the thirteenth of June, 1863, seven hundred, and on the twentieth of January, 1864, five hundred and sixty sick and wounded came in. These were the two largest single trains. On a cold midnight of December, 1863, two hundred and fifty badly wounded men from skirmishes in the Army of the Potomac crept wearily up. Then four hundred came in two days, and a hundred and eighty more at midnight of the second day.

Large numbers arrived in midsummer of 1864, many of them "Hundred Days men" broken down at once by camp sickness, and more exacting and discontented than any other class of patients. In a fortnight, or little more, of the May of 1865, after the "quick march home" which sounded so finely in the newspapers, we took in fourteen hundred and ninety men. There was now and then a general clearing out of convalescents for duty, a large number of transfers or discharges at once, or a sweep of "able" men in some sudden alarm for the safety of Washington. Generally speaking, however, the arrivals and departures were by small squads and happened every few days, so that it needed constant watchfulness to see that the comers and the goers were properly cared for in all respects.

Our alarms were never very serious, but every precaution was taken against their possible consequences. In September of 1862, after the Second Bull Run, a line of earthworks was thrown up a little outside the camp limits. In March of the next year a line connecting all the forts was finished and strengthened. A tidy little redoubt lay just on the edge of the grounds. In June a detachment of the Signal Corps escorted by a troop of horse took possession of the tower as a signal station, and the dipping of little flags by day and waving of colored lanterns by night was picturesque and curious. Fitz-Hugh Lee was reported at Annandale close by, with cavalry. In April of 1864, one hundred of our men of the Second Battalion, Invalid Corps, were suddenly marched away to take the place of "Augur's reinforcements" from the forts about Washington. In July the rebels advanced northward; Washington was "threatened" again; every convalescent able to march was sent off; sounds of cannon were heard and there were soft alarms among the ladies of the ward officers' mess on the subject of what they called the "Grillers." Guerillas were known, indeed, to be just at hand, and one agent, or delegate, or sympathizer, in a yellow duster, wandering off beyond the earthworks "for a walk," was popularly supposed to have been captured and eaten by them.

Once in the middle of the night we were awakened suddenly by the assembly call from one of the forts, startlingly clear in the deep silence, followed by a roll of drums. There was nothing to hear or see out of the window, in the sweet darkness, but the birds twittering softly and a sort of expectancy in air and sky. We listened long, but nothing came of the expectancy; nothing but the wonder of the dawn, and we thought no more of guerillas till six o'clock, when we learned that the garrison had turned out on some false fright. In days like these the wards were thinned; once we got down to ninety-seven patients and reported a large number of empty beds. A friend coming then to see us from the city and looking up and down the barracks, says the empty beds make a keener impression on her than if they were full of maimed and suffering men; they look so grim, so ready.

The Surgeon in Charge always notified us of arrivals, discharges, etc. "I send you," he writes on a slip of paper for the store-room, "a copy of order just issued by me,—transfer of a hundred men to Northern hospitals. I know you will want to be kind to some of these men." He told us to call his attention to any man who seemed to us a subject for discharge who might by chance have been overlooked, and made a conscience-matter of hurrying through the discharge papers as rapidly as possible.

"I could not fulfil your request today," he sends word, "because I had a pile of discharge papers on my table and did not feel justified in doing anything but making them out and sending them forward. Think how many sad wives and poor little children depend on my promptness in this duty. I wish I had two heads and four hands." The broken-down men were always eager to be discharged and sent home. Once only, a poor fellow said when I asked him about getting away: "It's but a poor home I leave to go to; I'd rather stop here till I die."

The arrival of a large ambulance train was almost always announced by a mounted courier in advance, and word came at once to store-room and kitchen, so that every preparation could be made. Strong soup, beef-tea, bread and butter, and milk-punch in vast caldrons were always ready, and all hands were notified to be on the spot to help lift the patients and distribute the food. When the work in kitchen and store-room on such an occasion was well over, the wards were visited to see if any one had been overlooked.

There was never a critical case in hospital on which G.'s intelligence was not brought to bear in some shape. On one of these nights a nurse came hurriedly up with the word: "There's a man dying in Ward —; we can't do anything for him." "Has he taken anything since he came in?" "No'm, can't eat nothin'; doctor says musn't give him no stimulants, stomach's too weak." "I'll have a look at him," says G.; and after the nurse goes out—"the surgeon doesn't know a bronchitis from a broken leg. There's not a man in that ward who ought to die. *If* he is dying, he is dying of starvation." She hunts up the doctor and asks if wine-whey, the lightest of stimulants, may be tried. Doctor didn't know what it was, but had no objection; "man couldn't live anyhow." The man took the cup full eagerly, was "out of danger" in the morning, got well,—the doctor directing the nurse to be very particular to "give him his wine-whey reg'lar,"—went back to the field and helped to take Richmond.

It was delightful to see what changes rest, clean clothes, and a few good meals often made. Miserable heaps brought in on stretchers might be found in a week's time sitting up in dressing-gowns with newspapers in their laps; and in a week more with paper collars and pomatum in their hair. These articles I am commissioned to buy; also patent hair dye. I have more than once bought patent hair dye for the wards. Gregory had hair and *barbe d'Afrique* of the reddest red our eyes endure. I never saw anything so red; it gave out light and heat; or so pink as his eyes and so milk-white as his complexion. He devoted the first moments of his convalescence to applying the preparation which is not a dye, but which instantaneously turned beard, hair, and eye-brows purple-black. The effect was horrible—spectral. He got no quarter in the wards, however, and returned, by streaks, to the more harmonious colors of nature.

Men sometimes came into hospital lost in delirium, or too deeply exhausted to give the home address, and so died. T. D. was brought in far gone in fever and speechless. In his pocket were found a red morocco Testament and a poor little note-book half soaked through with rain or swamp-damp, in which a few wandering pencil notes were still legible, and the little couplet—

> *"Not a sigh shall tell my story,*
> *Silent death shall be my glory."*

The discolored leaves said here and there: "Camp bank of James, I am on guard. The sun is very hot. Moved camp for the third time and went to digging. Another hot day; I am sick. July 14th—We are getting our pay to-day; I say we, but I am not getting any—digging wears out so many clothes. 16th— Another hot day; I am sick; I am hardly able to do anything.

We are here in the old camp again. Have had no letter for three weeks. On the march—sleeping out of doors. Lay in the rain all night—sick—don't know where I shall go. Marched again—lay out of doors—very wet—no shelter." Through a photograph of a dark, sad-eyed young girl, with the name Mary —— on the back of it, we communicated with his friends and saved for them a lock of light brown hair, fine, thick, and soft as a little child's.

The mother wrote from Wisconsin:

"It was with a sad heart that I read the contents of your letter to Mary telling her of the death of my son. I feel very thankful to you for your kindness, and oh! how much more will I be, if you will be to the trouble to send me the articles you spoke of and the lock of hair you mention in your letter. Please answer this at once."

The soldier-nurses deserve good words. Many of them were the most faithful and devoted of men. Clumsy and tender, kindly, eager, and heavy-handed, they did what they could. Only here and there one was found who was capable of drinking up the milk-punch and setting the scrambled eggs aside for private banquets, and boldly wearing the flannel shirt given him for a patient. Old Smith meets me on my morning visit and tells me that he thinks the doctor in M ought to give Williams more stimulants; that he has a discharging wound and faints after every dressing. I advise him to go and find the doctor and put the case to him. He comes back in glee with an order on the store-room for punch and porter. Old Smith's patients always do well. He had a son in the army who was wounded and died far away from home, "and then I couldn't stand it any longer, ma'am, and I went in myself, and now whenever I get a young fellow like Williams to take care of, it seems like as if I was a doing for my own boy and it a makes me feel better."

In another ward I encounter Vincent, who "spells it with a Wee," and who addresses me all in a breath: "Well, Miss — —, four doctors is after me for their wards but I think I'll stick by the old gentleman in the specs or Doctor Havens who as fur as I can see is a gentleman too. I objected to Doctor Davis though I won't say but what he's a nice little man enough I hated to give him up but them stairs and now when you see anything wrong in my ward don't you be afraid to say so though I do allow that my ward is the cleanest on the hill." "Wincent" endorses the Surgeon in Charge. "He's a quick man and a kind man," he says:—"He's a wiolent and a patient man—he'd get out of his bed and sick himself any time day or night to go and see a sick soldier me and him never had no words whatever."

Here is a wardmaster much elated with the importance of having small-pox break out in his ward, and a "difficult" one with whom I make an appointment to thread lint after his instructions, "for I want some much better than any kind of lint that ever came into this Hospital, ma'am."

We were often troubled by the changes and transfers among the detailed men and the need of teaching new sets of cooks and nurses. When three companies of the Invalid Corps came down to us, we thought these cares were over. Soon after their arrival, however, forty were discharged as perfectly useless. Then we began to fill in with transfers of our own men to the corps. Poor fellows! What with being terribly "chaffed" in the wards by the sick men who took this base advantage of their own weakness, and what with hating the corps and the strange officers and the dress parade, and above all things the toy sabres they carried, their lives were a burden to them. I did not see that changing the name to "Veteran Reserves" made matters much better. They could not bear to give up the comradeship and traditions of their own old regiments. "I came out with the Massachusetts 18th and now I'm to go home with a pig-sticker, and a pair of white cotton gloves!" If there was any disturbance in camp it was always "them Inv'lids." If the ward pet cat was killed or the apples stolen from the mess-hall kitchen it was "one of them Inv'lids." If a man hung about the stoves in the ward,—"oh, you're no good,—go and get yourself condemned for an Inv'lid." Disparaging doggrel was handed about, of which a verse or two from one "poem" may serve as a specimen:

> *O who are the men in skim-milk blue*
> *Who grumble and grumble the whole day through?*
> *"Too little to eat and too much to do?"*
>   *Them Inv'lids.*

> *Who "serve the country" in hunting rats?*
> *And stealing the chops from the kitchen vats?*
> *And docking the tails of harmless cats?*
>   *Them Inv'lids.*

> *Who hob and nob with their own commanders*
> *And converse like the British troops in Flanders?*
>   *Them Inv'lids.*

> *Who flourish swords like the Thane of Cawdor's*
> *And snap their fingers at General Orders?*
>   *Them Inv'lids. etc., etc,*

The ward medical officers, "Contract Surgeons," were more or less victims of a system which made them an anomalous civil element in a military establishment, with but little military restriction and no military incentive in the shape of promotion. They had no position, small pay, and mere nominal rank. They were a temporary expedient in the first place—and who shall say what better one could have been devised for the emergency?—but the emergency went by, and the expedient was stretched into a corps of fifteen hundred men to whose hands were committed the wards of almost all General Hospitals. They served their little term, made their little experiments and disappeared. The class was bad; it was under no bonds to be anything else; the exceptions were many and most honorable.

I have known a "contract surgeon for three months"—six months—refuse to attend a dying man, or attempt to ease his mortal agony because the patient was "no good anyhow" and the surgeon "had company." I have known one operate on the slightly injured member and let the shattered one go, and on being "relieved" for drunkenness, begin in a neighboring hospital a fresh career of cutting off your wrong leg; and one who recommended a man for field duty with two inches of the bone of his right arm gone, and explained by saying he was "sure he wouldn't have sent him up if he had only known it."

But I have also known contract surgeons faithful, sagacious, tender-hearted, carrying their professional skill and their professional honor into the meanest contraband hut at any hour of the day or night, spending day and night with their soldier patients, watching them, devising every manner of expedient for their relief; humoring their fancies, telling them cheerful stories, tending them like brothers and sons.

In the wards were representatives of many nations, Germans, Italians, French, Swiss, but the large majority were Americans, of New England and the West. There were loyalists from West Virginia and Tennessee, one or two stray rebel prisoners, a few blacks and three Chippewa Indians, sharpshooters from Michigan. One of these wanted a letter written to his mother, *Shawonega Pahwequa*, and on being asked to dictate, said, "Oh, say whatever you would say to your mother if you were sick." Besides all these, there was a strange soldier who drifted into the Hospital or rather was found there after some arrival, whose name, regiment, State and very language were utterly undiscoverable, and who remained an unsolved mystery, appearing everywhere in camp and silently presenting arms to the Surgeon in Charge whenever he passed, till that officer began to believe himself haunted by the ghost of some man in blue whom he had innocently aggrieved.

The sick were almost always patient and cheerful; only now and then one, utterly broken down, was despondent and peevish. The wounded men were marvels of good and even gay humor. An access of pain once over, they were actually jolly. McC. went across with the volunteer party in the boats to Fredericksburg and his thigh was shattered in storming the heights. He is an apple-cheeked, blushing boy, who "doesn't see as he did anything." Salmon, a noble man full of courage and patience, had the carotid artery tied after a gunshot wound of the jaw and throat. When asked if there is anything he wants he writes on the slate: "Only to get well and go at 'em again!"

The brothers Hinton lie side by side, the corporal and the sergeant, each with the right arm gone. They are very fine fellows, with frank, handsome faces of the Saxon sort, resolute for any treatment the Surgeon in Charge thinks necessary, light-hearted and merry over their games and arithmetic problems and practice of left-hand writing. Corporal Hooker, with the right arm amputated at the shoulder, says: "I want you to write to my mother and tell her she mustn't take on about it. She hasn't any right to feel worse than I do, and I guess I can stand it." The last we heard of the corporal he was offering to break his left arm over the head of a man at home who spoke disrespectfully of the service.

S. was a dear boy, patient, cheerful, and lovely-tempered. He was very anxious to get well, and faithfully followed all instructions. The nurses heard him softly praying in the night, "Dear Saviour, give me strength to see the morning." His serene temper was in his favor, and to the surprise of all he began to improve slowly and was able at last to get home. David W. died of fever and scorbutic disease, exhausted by long hardship and neglect. He was courtly even in his last agony. I fanned him a great deal, as he liked it, but he said repeatedly, "Your arm must be tired, pray don't tire yourself." "Do you like it?" I asked. "Oh, yes! It is delightful, but don't tire your arm for me. I couldn't bear that."

One wounded man was very sullen, poor fellow. He had the look of a city "rough." He said he had been "dragged about so since he was shot, he didn't believe he would ever be well." He "thought he should like a reg'lar novel." So I took him the "Arkansas Avengers"—sent by some good soul for just that use,—a chequer-board and a comic almanac, for all which he was very grateful. I wondered whether I ought not to try and elevate his tastes, but decided it was hardly fair to take the time when I had him helpless at my mercy. "Convalescents" were the most pitiable class. Illness is itself an occupation. These men, able to get about, but too weak and spiritless to do anything or care for anything, sickened by the sight of food in quantity, fretted to pain by noise and by the very light of day, thrust aside by busy nurses, rather condemned by surgeons as "lame-backs" and "good-for-nothings,"—how did they ever get through the long and weary hours?

The men were all fond of flowers. Hot-house flowers some-times came down to us, and the lovely white and crimson carnations, were a delight to a sick sergeant, who touched and fondled them, and had them fastened to the frame of the bedstead close by his head, and died with one clutched in his thin fingers. One spring morning I carried a bunch of the first lilacs to a very sick New England boy. "Now I've got something for you," I said, holding them behind me, "just like what grows in your front door-yard at home; guess!" "Lalocs!"—he whispered, and I laid them on his folded hands;—"oh, *lalocs!* How did you know *that*?" The lilacs out-lived him.

All classes of men were pleased with a little kindness, grate-ful for the smallest attention, always thanking us, each in his own way, from the long, solemn, lank-haired New Englander, who, just fitted out with home-made shirt and socks, writing materials, moral fiction and "jel," expressed the climate of his content in the words: "Wall, I aint got no complaints to make,"—to the blonde, blue-eyed German who called G. to his bedside one morning to tell her his dream of her. "Last night I dreamed," he said, "that I was walking by myself in a great city and came to a bridge over a deep river. As I crossed the bridge it broke and I fell into the water and was sinking, when you came and drew me to land. I was all dripping and you took me to your own house and gave me a whole new suit of clothes all dry and warm. Then you said: 'You may go into the garden and take a flower; take any flower you like.' So I took a rose; but as I was picking it I died and went to Heaven. You called aloud to me: 'Don't drop the rose; take it with you and plant it in Heaven for me.' So I went to Heaven and planted it, and it grew and blossomed. And when the blossoms came I sent you down word, and you died and came to Heaven and found there all ready a rose-tree, blooming for you."

The Frenchmen in the wards were always light-hearted, sweet-tempered, and graciously polite. Charmoille, with the right arm gone, taught himself an elaborate and beautiful manner of writing with the left hand, in the hope of getting some little clerkship when he should be discharged. Louis L., with amputation of the thigh, seemed to gain strength too slowly; so he was asked one day: "Is there nothing you think of that you would like,—that you used to like at home?" "O, Madame, I want for nothing; I have everything that one could desire." "But try and think of something that would do you good, and perhaps we can get it for you." "Ah! There is nothing, Madame; but—since you say it—two drops of red wine, *du vin de mon pays, Madame*;—but you could not— here in Virginia." With the cheerful consent of the surgeon a small ration of Burgundy was sent down every day, and with it poor Louis made a little daily fête of his dinner and sang a little song about not forgetting to pass the red wine and dying for the country all-so-gay. The *deux gouttes de vin rouge* seemed to brighten the whole ward.

Patrick D. was earning twenty dollars a week as an engineer when the war broke out. "Sure," he says, "I didn't see why I hadn't as good a right to fight for the country as the other boys." When his illness took a bad turn we sent for his wife, and she happily arrived in time, bringing a white, wailing baby which was laid in a soldier's empty bed in sight of the father who gazed on it with great content. "Sure you're all very good to me here," he says, "but I just put my head under the blanket and cry a little now and then about the five at home and no one to feed 'em when I am gone."

K. was a loyal Virginian of the 1st Virginia Volunteers. He was taken with fever, swept up with a crowd of others to make room for the wounded after a battle and shipped for the North where he had a relapse of typhoid and was very ill for many weeks. He was a tall, strikingly handsome fellow of twenty-three or four, with dark eyes and hair, regular, fine features, small feet and long, taper, beautiful hands. He was very careful of his clothes and personal appearance, and clamored for a tooth-brush and a "perfectly fresh" towel. His regiment had been badly thinned—"They are very hard on us loyal Virginians," he says;—"They call us traitors. Traitors indeed!" flushing and sparkling; "What are *they*? We were badly off at first; there were the rebels all among us; we had no arms; no supplies; no Governor Letcher didn't count; and they tormented us; but when we got a Governor and equipments they began to sing dumb." He scorned the idea of a discharge and went back to the field declaring "he would fight it out while he lived."

Prisoners and Prison Rings

W E HAD BUT ONE OR TWO REBEL PRISONERS in the wards, and very few National soldiers who had been in rebel hands. Hospitals nearer the sea-coast received this class of men. Now and then a returned prisoner came to us.

The first things these men wanted after food, was paper and ink to write home. Sometimes the happy letters came back from home before the soldier was furloughed. One wife wrote to her husband who had not been able to communicate with his family for nearly a year: "We were sitting round the stove reading Mr. ——'s speech about how Union prisoners are treated, when a knock came at the door and your letter was handed in. First I thanked and blessed God, and then I kissed the lines wrote by that dear hand I lost so long."

Hunter, a loyal Tennessean, told me the story of his enlisting, and gave me a little ring he had made in prison. What hospital nurse has not a bone riled or trinket carved by her men in the wards or in prison? Strung on this ribbon are specimens of the art in all its stages, from the plain boxwood circlet of the early days, through the inlaid foil and sealing-wax phase, to the period of delicately finished ornament in relief;

rings with a rose, a little cannon, a dog couchant, two clasped hands, an open book. Here are a Greek cross finished in roses, a Latin cross inlaid with black and the name of the Hospital; a cross pure white; the dear boy who made this, said to me before he died: "I thought of putting your initials on it, but I could not bring myself to put even yours on anything of that shape." Here is a scarf pin in the form of a shield with the word "Constancy" relieved on it in a garland of flowers. Here is a ring of hard wood made by a rebel prisoner. He modestly offered it in return for something given him, saying,—"I am a rebel, madam, but if you will take the ring"—What could one do but take the ring and make the wish that it might be a token of better days coming?

Hunter, the loyal Tennessean, told me the day he first sat up in his rocking chair, how he came to be a soldier. His home was in the hill country of East Tennessee. "They watched us a long time," he said; "me and some others. They thought we was a going for the Union. We had made up our minds what to do. One night we went off. We made for where we thought the army was." "What army?" I asked inadvertently. "THE ARMY," he repeated reprovingly; "there ain't but one." The National army was the only one to him. "The first night we spent in the woods. I laid the fire before I went. I laid her a good fire. At daylight we got to the top of the mountain, where we could look down at our homes behind us. They were getting up and lighting the fires. I saw my little house. The smoke was coming out of the chimney. She had to light it herself. I sat down on a flat rock and looked down into the valley. I wanted to see if the fire burned. Well! (with a long sigh) it was my home; I suppose it was as sacred to me as another man's home to him. I turned my back on it, me and the others. We travelled nine days and nights in the

woods, hiding days and travelling nights, and once we passed
the rebel picket with a cow-bell tied round Robert's neck, and
got to the army in Kentucky, and three days afterwards we
went in and took the Gap. We were taken prisoners there,
my brother and me, and went to Knoxville and then to Macon, and there I saw my dear brother die in the filth of the
prison and I not able to help him. After eight months we were
taken to Columbia and Salisbury, and then to Richmond and
after awhile to Aiken's Landing. I made this ring in Macon
jail. You see we had almost nothing to work with; and when
we made anything we put on it Union, or Forever, or two
clasped hands to mean *True till Death*, or something like that.
I wish you'd take the ring."

Let those who have one of these rings with two clasped
hands to mean "True till Death," keep it as a sacred relic. It is
the prison sign or fashion, a sad fashion that seemed to travel
underground and everywhere prevailed. I have had it from
Texas, Atlanta, Columbia, Belle-Isle, Andersonville. It is as
characteristic as the palm branch of the Catacombs.

With Hunter came Sergeant F——, of Michigan. He had
been sick in the prison in Georgia for nearly a year, and had
no care and no medicine except when he could sell a little of
his wretched food and buy some. "He kept up," he said, "and
kept moving about, for he observed that when a man once
gave out and lay down he didn't get up again."

Captain —— came to us direct from his imprisonment.
He was a young officer of refined education and habits, and
had "suffered many things" of the enemy. Such little preparation as we could command was made to do him honor. A
bath, a suit of clothes "a world too wide" belonging to one of
the officers, fresh linen, a delicate handkerchief, cologne and
toilet apparatus were set out in his little room. A modest

nosegay was folded in his napkin at dinner. At table he scarcely ate or spoke. He could not handle knife and fork. He seemed benumbed,—body and soul. He clumsily singled out a flower to put in his coat. Some one offered a pin to fasten it. He tried in vain to pick it up, and, stretching out his poor shrunken and stiffened fingers, pleaded: "Excuse me; it is so very small." After awhile he looked about cloudily, and said: "You are like angels. These—are the courts of Heaven."

Mail Days

A LARGE COLLECTION OF HOSPITAL LETTERS lies under my hand. Some of these are from men cured and sent back to the field. Some are from men on furlough, or wornout men discharged and sent home. Some are from transferred nurses, giving their experiences in other hospitals. Some, the most touching, are from friends at home, asking for news of their soldiers, or acknowledging tidings of illness or death. But they are all touching enough,—in the struggle for expression of persons not used to putting their thoughts on paper; the elaborate folding; the pathetic ill-spelling; the patriotic device, the red and blue edges of the sheet; sometimes in the perfect correctness and delicacy of the little document in all its parts. Some are restrained and quiet; some are full of noble courage and patience; some are the pouring out of helpless love and sorrow. So many beg for further particulars; "Write more;" "Tell me everything ;" "What did he say of *me*?" "He must have left some word about the children;" "If I could only know his thoughts as he went away from earth." I take a few of them up at random.

Very early in the war a father writes:

MY DEAR MISS ——

I am very glad to know by your writing that my son died among Christians instead of among rebels. My only fears are that he had not the care when he was first taken sick he ought to have had. There are many stories that the sick are not well cared for in many places. I am sure that had any one known *how good my son was,* they could not have misused him. I should like to know what he said about his home, and also how he was buried. My son is dead,— through this rebellion. If I, his father, were Abraham Lincoln, I would kill the cursed cause of it, slavery, before many suns went down. Write all particulars of my son's death and relieve broken hearts.

E. T.

And a sister:

DEAR MISS ——

Will you be so kind as to give the enclosed letter to my brother. I have not heard from him since we parted, and it would give me both pleasure and courage to know how he is situated. I am taking a liberty, but I have heard persons say that you too have a brother in the army, and would be more apt than another to understand the anxiety of a sister's heart.   A. M

This mother is more anxious for her son's honor than for his safety or her own relief:

——, *New York; June 5.*

DEAR MADAM,

I am glad to hear from you that my boy is better. Do you a think he is likely to be soon strong enough to rejoin his regiment, or would it be better for him, as he is so young, to return home? I am anxious to know, too, what character he bears as a soldier. I cannot think he is strong enough for the hardships of camp life, but as I have his own honor at heart more than my desire to see him again, I hesitate to apply for his discharge.

Julia M.

William H. was furloughed, and in a few days, from far up in the country, came a little box with eggs packed in oats, and butter-pats wrapped in linen and broad green leaves. He had learned to knit in hospital, and made two wonderful and beautiful pairs of fine, red stockings, for the shaping of which he borrowed one of ours, and insisted on giving them to us as a parting present. The occupation was good and the idea seemed to give him constant amusement; the turning of the table; a sick soldier knitting socks for a lady. He writes:

RESPECTED FRIEND,

I write to say that I have sent by express a small box with a few eggs for your own private use and a little print of butter for your own use, and some for the other ladies. I want to send you some little notion from home, and thought this was the best I could send. I feel a desire to hear from the Hospital how you all are. Remember me to the Chaplain. I trust the Lord will bless his labors. I feel a great desire to see you all, and enjoy a day or two at the Hospital. I hope your life will be precious in God's sight. I have not been so well since I got home, and get low-spirited and nervous, but when I review the past and see how God's Providence has been around me, I feel to thank Him and take courage.

Your grateful friend,
William H.

What a characteristic story is this; what glimpses of a noble soul!

March 31, 1864.

My Dear Miss ——

When I first opened your letter I dared not look at the commencement, but glanced my eye toward the bottom and read: "Your dear husband had good care during his illness." I tried to think he was better. I jumped up and clapped my hands, and said, "Oh! it's news from John." I sat down and began to read again until I read, "At half-past eight God took him:" when I fell to the floor. Little did I think when he left his family that he never would return to them on earth. At the time he enlisted the recruiting officer promised him a furlough of eight days, but after he had been at New London a day or two, he was, with others, sent away without coming home. When he wrote to me from Philadelphia, he said: "*It is all right*; if it were not, God would not permit it to be so." After he made up his mind to volunteer he seemed perfectly happy and said his duty in life was only just begun. The night after he went I taught Frankie a new prayer,—"God take care of my dear papa,"—and little Rosa has learned it too. I can never see you or thank you for your kindness to him. If I could know what his thoughts were as he went away from earth!   J. B.

Letters often came into the Superintendent's hands after the death of the soldier. A young sister says:

——, *Indiana, Oct. 9, 1864.*

Dear Brother,

We wrote yesterday and the day before, so there is not much to write, only that mother wants you to keep up good cheer. You will get this on your birthday, and mother says she wishes she could get there with it. She says if you feel sad and lonely you must look to God for comfort. She feels almost too nervous to try and write tonight.

Minnie ——

Another letter, found in the pocket of a dead man, is from his wife and says that her landlord has threatened to turn her out with her little children into the cold, and begs her husband to come home and see her and the children and get some shelter for them.

It was frequently a painful task to decide whether friends should be summoned; whether there was need of it; whether there was time. These friends were often poor and burdened with the care of children, and the journey was often long.

——, *New Hampshire, Jan. 27, 1864*

DEAR MISS ——

I received yours of the 21st last evening. I thank you very much for writing about my husband. Please read him the enclosed if he is not able, and will you write me as soon as you get this, and ask him if he thinks it best for me to come? Tell me just what he says. Tell me just what is thought about him. I want to know the worst. I ask you again to write as soon as you get this. If he expresses the least wish I will start immediately. I shall be so disappointed if I do not hear again this week. I am so anxious about him.

A.G.

Furloughed:

——, *January 26, 1863.*

In compliance to your request, I write to say that I got home on the 17th and found my family well. How glad to be at home again! And we feel thankful to our Heavenly Father for his care over us during my absence, so that at our family altar we feel to say when I review the dangers and escapes I was in, that goodness and mercy have followed me all the days of my life and that He has covered my head in the day of battle. I can never forget you. My daily prayer is that God will spare your life to labor for the poor soldier. The day never passes but I think of the many favors received from Surgeon in Charge and officers. I was nowhere since I left home where I felt so satisfied as at the Hospital. May the Lord bless you and all those who labor with you, and at last may you hear the sweet voice of your Saviour say, "Inasmuch as ye have done it unto the least of these, ye have done it unto me."

Wm. W.

Furloughed:

——, *Wyoming County, N. Y., Dec. 14, 1863.*

MY DEAR FRIEND,

This is to inform you that I arrived at home on the 12th. We stayed at the Soldiers' Home in New York, so it cost us nothing. I got home next day and took them by surprise. You can imagine how happy we were. I think she looked a little older, though not so sad as when we parted. I was much fatigued, but think I shall be better in a few days. I can never half thank you for all your kindness while I was there.

G.C.

I think she looked a little older. Who shall tell the story of the women at home, or measure the hope and the fear and the "constant anguish of patience?"

These are sons and fathers worthy of each other:

———, *Wisconsin, July 29, 1863.*

DEAR MISS ———

I take my pen to let you know that I received your kind but distressing letter telling of the death of my dear son. But he fell on the field, defending his country! My stranger friend, I am happy to think you respected my son to take such care of him during his illness. I hope you will answer this letter and give me more particulars about his death, and if he said anything about anything at home, or if he mentioned any of the family, or if he said anything about dying, and *if he was buried with the honors of war.* But I have said all that I can say by thanking you a thousand times, and bring my letter to a close by asking God to bless you.

C. S.

No man was buried without the "honors of war," as prescribed in the Army Regulations. The colonel of a raw regiment encamped near by, once complained to the Surgeon in Charge that the firing over the grave made his men "nervous" and begged him to discontinue it, but without avail.

———, *N.Y. Oct. 13, 1863*

MISS ———

Yours of the 8th was received informing me of my son Lorenzo's death. Great as is his loss to me yet from the tone of your letter I feel reconciled to the will of our Divine Master. I have four sons in the Federal Army; would I had four more. I would give them freely, hoping for their welfare and trusting in God. God's Will be done. In your letter, you wrote you wanted to write more fully soon. Do so, and let me know if he was conscious of his situation, his last words and feelings, and all his sayings in his last hours. Should you know of anything whieh may have been desired by him, please inform me.

B.M.

———, *Ohio, Feb. 25, 1864.*

DEAR BROTHER,

We received your letter to-day. Father says you must take good care of yourself. He says he is going to keep a pair of white-faced oxen for you. Mother says the time seems long since she saw you. She wants you to take care of your health and be a good boy. She wants you to write once a week certainly. If you want anything you can't get, let us know, and we will try to get it for you. Give our best respects to Luke if he is there. I will get you some good story papers.

Annie H.

Private H. languished and died in Hospital; the mother at home counting the time long since she saw her boy, and the "white-faced oxen" waiting in the stalls.

What a noble and pathetic letter is this last in the handful! The father and the Mother write:

———, *N. Y., March, 1864.*

DEAR FRIEND,

We feel very thankful to you for the respect you have shown our dear son. We feel to bless God that he raised up such good friends. We felt you did all you could for our son, and more for being so kind as to write to us and let us know where are laid his mortal remains. You wrote you thought he was praising God. It was the greatest comfort to us of anything. To think that we shall one day meet where there is no war, no enemies, no blood and carnage; where our suffering is all done with! We should like to know if Amos bore it patiently. He was always very patient at home. We are old and infirm. It was hard parting with him when he left home. It seems sometimes that I could almost hear him praising God and beckoning. It will not be long. We will pray for you in your station, and for those who administered to the wants of our son. We feel for others as well as ourselves. *We are not alone by thousands.* We have one son left; he has lost part of his hand; and one son-in-law with Banks. We would like to know if Amos said anything about his friends. Was it so that he could not talk much? How did his mind appear to run? It seems he would have said something about his father; he always thought so much of him. Was his mind on prayer or on the Bible? He wrote to me that if he fell he should fall safe. He said he prayed for us and for himself. But his place is vacant. But we have One to go to who can be touched with our infirmities. If you think of anything more let us know. We should be glad of anything more.

From your friends George —— and Lucy ——,
His father and mother.

On the 12th of May, 1864, keeping a standing engagement with the Sanitary Commission, G. got a furlough of a few days and went to Fredericksburg; and presently, into the order and comfort of the Hospital came, in sharp contrast, two or three letters from her, written on odd leaves of paper, mercilessly abbreviated in every other word.

Belle Plain, Va., May 13, 1864.

On the S. C. boat, pulling up to the shore Government flatboats of horses and cavalry recruits. There are no docks and the army supplies are being landed from barges connected by pontoons with the shore. A constant stream of contrabands passing with bags of grain and barrels of pork on their shoulders. Dr. Douglas and Dr. Agnew are here. Good Dr. Cuyler is here. Senator Pomeroy is on board going down to bring up General Bartlett of Massachusetts, who went into the fight with a Palmer leg and was wounded again. Col. —— tells me there has been great anxiety at the War

Department. Mr. Stanton said to him: "When we have a victory the whole North shall know it." "And when there is silence?" said Col. ———. "Then," said the Secretary,—"there is no communication with the front." We have a Feeding-Station on shore and are putting up another two miles away, on the hill, where ambulance trains halt sometimes for hours, owing to obstructions in the road. The mud is frightful and the rain is coming on again. We are directed to take the return train of ambulances for Fredericksburg.

Just as I finished, the train from Fredericksburg arrived. Nothing I have ever seen equals the condition of these men. They had been two or three days in the ambulances; roads dreadful; no food. We have been at work with them from morning till night without ceasing; filling one boat, feeding the men; filling another, feeding them. There is no sort of use in trying to tell you the story. I can scarcely bear to think of it. All the nurses and cooks from the Invalid Corps of our Hospital, who marched off that day, Sullivan, Lewis and the rest, armed with muskets again, are down here guarding prisoners. Yesterday a squad of rebel officers was marched on board a boat lying by ours. I had to pass through their ranks to get supplies from our boat, and shook hands with our boys and saw the officers; Stewart and Bradley Johnson among them; strong, well-fed, iron looking men, all of them. There's no "give in" in such looking men as these. Our soldiers from the front say the rebels stand—stand—in solid masses, giving and taking tremendous blows and never being shoved an inch. It is magnificent!

No words can express the horrible confusion of this place. The wounded arrive one train a day, but the trains are miles long; blocked by all sorts of accidents, wagon trains, bad roads, broken bridges; two, three days on the way, plunged in quagmires, jolted over corduroy, without food, fainting, starving, filthy; frightfully wounded, arms gone to the shoulder, horrible wounds in face and head. I would rather a thousand times have a friend killed on the field than suffer in this way. It is worse than White House, Harrison's, or Gettysburg by far. Many die on the way. We found thirty-five dead in the ambulances yesterday, and six more died on the stretchers while being put on board the boats. The boats are anything that can be got hold of, cattle scows, anything. Barges of horses are landed by the side of the transports and the horses cross the deck where the helpless men lie. Mules, stretchers, army wagons, prisoners, dead men and officials as good as dead are tumbled and jumbled on the wretched dock, which falls in every little while and keeps the trains waiting for hours. We fed the men at once. We fed all the five boats that got off yesterday. There is no Government provision for this, beyond bread; no coffee, no soup, no cups or pails, or vessels of any kind for holding food. The men eat as if starving. These had been three days without food. We are ordered to Fredericksburg to-day to report to Dr. Douglas, as there is more misery there than here.

Fredericksburg, Va., May 19, 1864.

All right. Hard work, dirt and death everywhere. Mrs. Gibbons arrived last night. She and her daughter are assigned to a fearful place, where they are working hard. I am in the Feeding-Station. Men are continually brought in and stowed away in filthy warehouses called distributing-stations, where for three or four days no one in particular seems responsible for them. They are frightfully wounded and die in numbers in the stations. No provision whatever for feeding them is made by Government, beyond hard-tack and coffee. We go about among them and feed them. I have good men as assistants and can have more. I have a room of special cases near by, besides the general station. Three of these died last night. Care came too late. They had been several days on the field after being shot; in and out of the enemy's hands; taken, retaken. Mr. Clarke of Paris and Mr. Thaxter are busy everywhere; Mr. Clarke with a tear in his eye and a rose in his button-hole. More straw stealing, corn-shuck stealing, plank stealing (the townspeople refuse to sell and we steal everything we can lay our hands on for the patients); more grateful, suffering, patient men; more dirt and unnecessary shifting about of the wounded.

May 22.

Dr. Buck and Dr. Markoe went this morning. Dr. Clark of Boston is still here. More like these three gentlemen would have been an unspeakable blessing. Orders about transportation of wounded have been given and countermanded and given again. Tent hospitals have been put up and then surgeons ordered not to fill them. No confusion was ever greater. Orders came from Washington that the railroad should be repaired—why was it not done ten days ago and the wounded sent by it? Then orders came withdrawing guard from railroad. The Medical Department refused to send wounded over an unguarded road. Telegram from Washington that wounded should go by boat. Telegram back that trains of wounded were already over the pontoons, ready to go by railroad if protected. Telegram that they should go by boat. Trains come back to boat. River falling; rumors of blockade. One boat full got painfully off. Second boat off. Ambulance trains at many hospital doors. Go round and feed the worst cases for embarking. Get on an ambulance of the train and feed some poor fellows with eggnog; one, shot through the lungs, one, through thigh, and move on with the slow-moving procession,—at every moment a jolt and a "God have mercy on me!"—through the darkness, over the pontoons, to the *railroad* again.

The moving of the men is what no one likes to think of. No selection is made; such and such places are "cleared" without regard to cases, and every day six or eight men are taken out of the ambulances at Belle Plain dead, who would have lived if they had been quiet, while the city is full of men slightly hurt.

I cooked and served to-day 926 rations of farina, tea, coffee, soft crackers and good, rich soup, chicken, turkey and beef, out of those blessed cans. The great confusion in regard to government feeding of the men in Fredericksburg, after the difficulty of getting up enough food over the road, comes from the stupid division of the hospitals into so many parts. Each little shop full, or room full, or collection of wounded men has a surgeon, usually civilian contractor. He reports to the surgeon in charge of the *group* of rooms, shops, etc. This officer reports to surgeon of division; surgeon of division, to corps surgeon; corps surgeon draws on the commissary for number of rations he needs for the day. The rations are divided and sub-divided; so much for corps, so much for division, so much for each hospital, and then the wardmaster for each hospital takes the food in the rough and has it cooked, and all the little shops and rooms send and get it in tin cups and old pails. It has often been ten o'clock at night before "dinner was ready," and when you consider that many of these men require feeding every hour or two, you may easily see how important have been the "irregular" supplies of the Sanitary Commission and other organizations.

We are lodged with a fine old lady, mild and good, in a garden full of roses. We board ourselves. We have crackers, sometimes soft bread, sometimes beef. We have plenty and are well. Last night we had a slice of ham all round. The wounded are being removed. The town will be deserted in a few days. We are sweeping and cleaning Mrs.———'s rooms to leave the old lady as well off as we can, for all her servants have packed their feather-beds and frying-pans and declare they will go with us.

Having a moment of leisure, G. wrote once more, and this time it was about the roses in Fredericksburg:

Augur's reinforcements have passed through. As the troops
went forward along the street, they were met by the ambulances
of wounded from the front, who thrust out their poor hands and
waved and weakly cheered them. Mrs. ——'s house has a large,
old-time garden full of roses; indeed, the whole town is brimming
with early flowers. We begged and received permission to take all
we could gather, and filled our baskets, trays, and the skirts of our
gowns, with snowballs, lemon-blossoms, and roses—yellow, white,
and red. The 8th New York Heavy Artillery was in the column. In
the headstall of Colonel Peter Porter's horse we fastened a knot
of roses, and tossed roses and snowballs in showers over the men.
They were delighted. "*In Fredericksburg!*" they said; "Oh, give me
one;"—"Pray give me one ;"—"I will carry it into the fight for you;"
and another cheerily,—"I will bring it back again!"

Three days afterwards the ambulances came; and in them came
some of the same men, shattered, dying, dead. We went out, but
this time it was with pails of soup and milk-punch. One and another recognized us; all were cheery enough. "A different coming
back, ma'am."—"No roses to-day!"—and one said, pointing over
his shoulder: "The Lieutenant is there on the stretcher, and he's
brought back the flowers as he promised." I went to the side, hoping to help a wounded man. The Lieutenant lay dead, with a bunch
of dead roses in the breast of his coat.

A woman-nurse, transferred to a General Hospital farther
North, writes of her experience:

I have one hundred men in my ward, all in bed. The surgeons
appear to give very little care to the diet, but are down on any one
else who does. The food is very poor and insufficient. The cooks
seem to have it all their own way. The ladies are not allowed to
superintend in the kitchen or have anything to do with it. For thirty-

eight of my men the ward surgeon orders, in general terms, milk and eggs. It is grimly amusing to hear him say day after day, "milk and eggs for thirty-eight." One egg apiece, each meal, is all I can ever get from the cooks, and for two days there have been no eggs at all. The milk rations are always short. At least once a day a clean sweep is made by someone, of all the light diets; so all that these thirty-eight men, many of whom are fearfully exhausted, have often had from the Hospital, has been a little rice, which they can't bear, and a slice of bread. No steak and potatoes, no egg-nog, no milkpunch, nothing generous whatever comes into the ward.

All this wears upon one infinitely more than the hard work. What shall we give in place of the missing eggs? How shall we make up these miserably scanty rations? I have opened a private account at the village store for bread, butter, eggs, and milk enough for the ward, and we shall provide brandy and whiskey for the punches. I am told to "exercise my own judgment" in giving these out. No stimulant list has ever been furnished me. Our ward surgeon has gone to a horse-race which seems to be a pretty long one, and a strange surgeon looks in now and then.

The Surgeon in Charge seems kind in manner, visits the wards and attends to serious operations himself. He appears to do his part in the routine of the Hospital, drawing rations, issuing them to the stewards, etc., strictly according to regulations, but seems to think that stewards are the best persons to manage the food business. The Hospital fund could and should provide everything. The object of the minor officers seems to be to subsist the men on nothing and avoid making a row. All that we women can do is to keep up a steady glare with the "eye of justice," and that, I assure you, we do. Our own quarters are poor, cold and leaky. For three nights we have been all crowded together, while wash-tubs, standing in the places of the beds, caught the rain beating in through walls and roof.

A set of regulations was promulgated this *P.M.* regarding female nurses, of which I give you as a specimen, *Number Five*: "All deliberations, discussions, and remarks having the object of expressing comparative praise or censure of the medical officers of this Hospital, or of their individual course or conduct, are positively prohibited." The provision against our praise is truly judicious!

But the worst of it is, we cannot keep the men alive. Eleven of mine have died in three days. Our usual three died last night from what the Chaplain facetiously calls the "dying corner." This officer's ministrations are something in this style: "Do you believe in a future state? yes; well; ah; then you hope for better things; then; ah; yes; you will die happy; good morning, brother." This to a man who thinks he is getting well is something of a damper. This afternoon, Sunday, he made a few remarks to the effect that death was waiting for them all, prolonging the subject till the usual afternoon funeral passed by, and bringing it in neatly: "Even now one of your comrades is being carried to the grave."

Another woman-nurse writes:

New York, July, 1864.

I went to —— General Hospital yesterday, to try and find K—— a transferred man. The Hospital is well situated, and the wards are comfortable and neat. The glare outside was painful, but the rooms were well ventilated, and there were plenty of flowers. Some ladies drove up with a carriage load of little bouquets, while I was there, and went about distributing them among the sick. They brought custards and jellies, too; but these were turned back at the door, and ordered to the steward's room. So I thought I would wait for dinner and see what they had. All the men in K.'s ward were in bed. At the twelve o'clock bugle, with great punctuality, two men came in, carrying a long plank between them. Ranged along the plank were bits of newspaper. On every bit of newspaper lay a thick slab of coarse bread, and on every slab of bread a cold boiled potato and a lump of fat "as big as my two thumbs," whether pork-fat or beef-fat, I could not tell. One of the newspaper plates was slipped on the table, or laid upon the counterpane of each sick man; knives and forks were distributed, and "dinner was ready."

I passed up and down that ward after awhile, and made a calculation with my eye. Fifteen men hadn't touched the repulsive meal. One said: "I can manage the bread and the potatoes; but who could eat that fat?" And another responded: "That's so;" and, tossing aside his flowers: "You can have all the posies if you'll get me a good square meal once more."

We wrote many letters for the men. These differed curiously sometimes. One young fellow very badly hurt wishes it said that he is "bully," and will be "round in a few days." Another, slightly wounded, dictates a fearful epistle to his friends, evidently meaning to "make their flesh creep":—"So they put me on the table, blood and bones sticking out in every direction," etc. "But shan't I add that you are better now?" "Well never mind that," says the hero. The indignation of an old Irishman on being asked if he wanted to write to his wife, was droll, but rather justified by the style of her last letter to him: "My cherished husband, it is with intense sorrow that I hear you are wounded. I never expected to see you more. I thought by this time your blood like others of your countrymen was watering the soil of Virginia," etc., etc. He presented the letter to G., saying he had no use for it.

These are from the parcel labelled "letters from the field;" they are from six or eight different soldiers and are

taken in the order of their dates. All show more or less of
the men and the time:

April, 1862.

The brandy and other things you gave me just before going off
were very valuable. A soldier of the 5th Maine, on picket with us a
few nights ago, was struck by a ball which broke his leg. He crawled
through the rain and cold of that miserable night, half a mile, on
his hands and knees to the reserve picket, and was just fainting when
I came up with the brandy treasured for just such a moment. I hope
we shall not be cheated out of a good fight. I hope J. and F. will
contrive to have a good fight.

Poor boys, they were at it already, thinking it would be all
over in sixty days:

Co. 6,——N.Y.Vol., July 6, 1862.

We are watching with fearful earnestness the operations before
Richmond. With what a will we gave "three times three," when the
Colonel told us on parade that he had heard from reliable, though
not official sources that Richmond is ours; how dreadful the shock
when we found McClellan had fallen back, losses 15,000, and it was
very little comfort that our army is in a better position for a fight
than ever. I ought not to call in question the doings of my superiors,
but it seems as if everything were put back for weeks.

Near Falmouth, Va., 23 January 1863.

On the 20th the greater part of Hooker's and Franklin's Divi-
sions began to march up the river, to cross and fight the "final deci-
sive battle" which McClellan forgot to fight on the Chickahominy.
Then came the dreadful storm of wind, rain, and sleet of the night
of the 20th, lasting till now. After struggling with mud for forty-

eight hours the whole expedition is countermarching miserably; stragglers by thousands; the road strung along with guns and wagons; everybody wet, miry, cold, hungry, and dreary. Just before this last movement some thousands of sick were sent to Aquia Creek. When they got there they found little or no provision made for them; so in a few days nearly all were sent back, some almost dying. They returned here in the midst of the storm with orders to "rejoin their regiments;" their regiments meanwhile had marched away. I begin to long a little for a short deliverance. If we were only always fighting and marching—but muddy camps are tiresome. We have read the testimony before the McDowell and Porter court-martial, the Prince de Joinville and Gurowski. The sun is coming out. I will go out and dry in it.

What could we do here without the Sanitary Commission? Many of our medicines, our stimulants, blankets, bedding, etc., for the field hospital come from the S. C. I would rather have Mr. Olmsted's fame than that of any General in this war since the beginning. Direct to me, Co. ——, —— N. Y. Vols.

Camp, August 7, 1863.

We are sweltering in the middle of a large field in a full glare of the hottest sun. Our camps are selected in this way: an officer takes a thermometer and casts about for the hottest spot and there the flag is planted. Our tent is at "water boils." We are delighted to see the draft progressing and hope we shall soon have large batches of men, *and one more campaign will finish up the war.*

October 9, 1863.

The drafted men come in by driblets, but like the "little drops of water" may in time make a swelling flood. So far they only make up for sick men and men on detached service. When they first began to come there was a disposition to make fun of them, but now we take very kindly to each other. They look as new and clean as the Seventh New York did in Maryland. The other day when a batch arrived, the place was full of loafers and a band was playing. "If I'd a'known it was like this, I'd a'come long ago," one of them said. I hope he'll say so the first time he charges on a battery. No furloughs are granted now, except under extraordinary circumstances. John Doyle sent up yesterday with his application the telegram he had from home: "Phil and Sophy are dead and the four others are expected to die." He got his fifteen days.

Many of the drafted men and substitutes who found their way to us in Hospital, at this time and later, were of the most worthless character, mere bounty-swindlers and refuse of foreign countries. One lost in their unblushing frauds all pity for their hopeless disability. One man in our camp, for instance, who had received nearly a thousand dollars in bounties and had been two months in the service, applied to his ward surgeon for discharge on the ground of epileptic fits of fourteen years standing. These, mother and wife, were the men who came down to stand beside your

"*Stainless soldier on the walls.*"

Some in their heroic deaths made us forget their shameful lives; many deserted; a few, let us hope, went home better men; hundreds drifted into hospitals, were discharged and re-enlisted for another bounty elsewhere. The men who "stood the draft" and came down were of a far better class than the substitutes. Now and then there was a curious case among these. S—— H——, of New Hampshire, was drafted in May, 1864, sent to Concord, thence to Boston Harbor, to Alexandria, and to Camp Distribution near Alexandria. He was then set to work on Arlington Heights fortifications, taken ill and sent to us. From us he was sent to Cliffburne barracks to be examined for the V. R. C., was declared unfit for the corps and returned to us. Never having been assigned to any regiment, he could draw neither pay nor clothes. He had eight children. He was an excellent, faithful nurse, being put on that duty in the Hospital and doing it admirably. The Sanitary Commission afterwards arranged the case and secured pay for the time he had been; in service, and he went home rejoicing.

In Camp, 6th April, 1864.

Grant has not pulled us out of the mud yet. I think the "side issue" at Fort Monroe must have been only a trip to see how the land lies. If it lies as loose and moist as it does here, he certainly doesn't mean fight. Dr. H. came down to stay over Sunday, and preach to us soldiers, but he addressed his city congregation. "You who see every day in the streets and shops"—much we do!—"and in your own comfortable dwellings," etc., or, "There is no child before me too young to," etc., etc. General Sheridan, said to be a first-class cavalry officer, has come to Headquarters. Great things are expected of him. He is said to be an ordinary-looking little man, who tells with a peculiar accent how well his men "done" in the West.

South of Germanna Fort, May 5, 1864

We have had probably the hardest fight of this campaign. Our losses have been great, for the fighting on both sides was desperate. But all goes well, and we are in good spirits, and confident of finishing up the thing this time. The ground is the very worst kind for fighting, a perfect wilderness of dense forests and underbrush where you would suppose it impossible for anything to get through. Your note reached me to-day when the musketry was very loud. Hurrah for the American eagle!

May 16, 1864

I can't begin to give you any account of the fight at Spottsylvania. We are resting after hard marching and fighting, and waiting for more men; some have come. While the enemy cannot make good his losses we shall fill up the gaps by Augur's men. We have whipped the enemy. Don't say, "Why don't they follow it up?" Remember that to follow it up rapidly and destroy such an army as Lee's, through this country after nine days of hard fighting, is simply impossible. There has been a large amount of straggling. The weary marches through the mud after hard fighting during the day, have done much of this. They are scattered and lost through the woods. We are in great straits for rations, but hopeful and in good spirits. "Ain't I glad" to be out of the Wilderness! A little way from our camp we see the enemy's line—a dirt-colored human fence against the green trees.

June 30, 1864.

We are on the left near the Weldon R. R., and are looking for news from Lynchburg. If Lee would only come out and fight—the army above all things desires it. We are marching in intolerable heat and dust, building miles of works, fighting day and night, never relieved and never safe from bullets. Sometimes I have lain down at night on the ground feeling that I could endure it no longer. Then I go and get behind the breastworks and listen to the talk so full of hope that one can't help feeling better for it.

In Camp, September 4, 1864.

The convalescents and recruits come in slowly. They are often improperly marched and give out on their way to their regiments and have to be returned to hospital. Poor little squads of companies now make up some of the regiments. Company commanders, corporals, have been heard to say: "Fall in, Company A. Fall in, men;

both of you." It is rumored there will be fighting to-morrow, owing to Early's return from the Valley. I suppose if we have had the great victory that is rumored we shall know it soon. As for McClellan, no matter what personal friendship may exist for him among the soldiers, I don't see how a soldier can endorse the Chicago platform. I cannot think that the people of the North mean anything but a continuance of the war until it is finished in the entire subjugation of the South. The soldiers have never known General McClellan in the dress he now wears. I, for my part, don't want to think I have spent two years in the army for nothing at all. We are to have a national salute in honor of Atlanta to-night.

September 9, 1864.

Yesterday some of the men of both sides were stealing out between the lines to talk and trade together, exchanging papers and comparing views on politics and the war. They had a little dog for mail-carrier, and wrote each other notes in loving terms as "My dear Johnny Reb," or "My dear Yank," in which they compared the price of cheese and tobacco, and enclosed the orders of the General inviting deserters. There is no sign of discouragement out here. It is like the old times of 1861. The adherents of McClellan are dropping off daily.

Camp 120th —— Vols., Feb. 12, 1865.

It is a bleak, desolate day, and we are at work building for the third time this winter our little city of logs. I cannot understand what we have accomplished by the week of fighting and exposures to which another week must be added before we can be comfortable, unless it is a diversion in favor of Sherman. When we came away the two chapels were none too large; the Dinwiddie Literary Association was a capital institution. Then we had every Thursday evening a general singing exercise, a class in the rudiments of music two afternoons a week, a Bible-class, and an old-fashioned spell-ing-class in prospect. It is to the chapel that my heart turns back most regretfully. It was unhewn and rude, but Ruskin might well enough mention it along with the mediæval cathedrals as an illus-tration of the Lamp of Sacrifice, for it was built as to the Lord, with a loving spirit. By the end of the week we hope to have a new chapel up, though by the end of the week we may have made an-other move by the left flank.

Hilton Head, S. C., Feb. 3, 1865.

One of the regiments here is the 3d U. S. C. T., the Inspector says, the best drilled of the Colored Troops, with as much snap in the manual of arms as any white troops he has seen. The orderly-sergeant of one company was a field hand, slave, five months ago; now he keeps all the company books in excellent condition. The 103d, recruiting here, is made up altogether of men who were slaves, who came into our lines in the wake of Sherman. We heard of the evacuation of Charleston last night. The ships in the har-bor made a show of fire-works.

12 Miles From Farmville, Va., 8th April, 1865.

It is hard to realize that the rebels are at last pushed to the wall, and that it is quite probable that Lee will surrender tomor-row. If you could have heard and seen the Sixth Corps marching through Farmville last night you would think they alone could finish up the rebellion—and they could. We have outrun our wagon train two days and nights. The roads are full of the wreck of Lee's army and his men are hustled to the rear by hundreds. They say that 10,000 have thrown away their muskets in the woods. Who would have thought ten days ago that things would come to this pass!

Appomattox C. H., 10th April, 1865.

We find it hard to realize the state of things; no Army of Northern Virginia; no lines beyond which it is dangerous to pass; no enemy! A lot of our men taken by them came back last night. I looked for G. among them. I hear he is all right. They gave our men for rations three ears of raw corn, each day. That Johnston will surrender and that *the end of the war has really come,* we do not doubt. It is a good thing to have had a part in this wonderful campaign.

City Point, Va., April 12, 1865.

It has been a tiresome march, but think of the results! A long column of prisoners coming in, with Custis, Lee, Ewell, and other rebel Generals at its head. We shall probably start for Richmond today.

April 24, 1865.

I trust General Grant will set General Sherman on the right track again. How he could ever have been switched of at such an angle I cannot imagine. Think of the rebels walking off to their State arsenals with their guns in their hands. It would be a surrender of Sherman to Johnston, instead of the other way. I think the Sixth Corps will encamp in the neighborhood of the Hospital soon.

This letter comes from the field accompanied by a gorgeous blue and gold photograph book, bought of some wretch of a camp sutler at an exorbitant price:

Camp Before Petersburg, July 1864.

ESTEEMED FRIEND,

A proposal was agreed on between Corporal F. and me last winter to present you with a suitable present worthy of your kindness to us, but owing to Corporal F. being sent home on furlough, it was put off. Then, I had joined my regiment, and we had no time to do anything owing to the campaign we have just passed through. The Corporal is in —— Hospital. I have been through the campaign with only slight bruises for a wonder, as the boys of the company say that I cannot go into battle without being wounded. I am expecting a commission this month. I am confident of a speedy success over the rebellion. I am in good spirits and determined to do my duty. Our regiment has behaved with great gallantry, though our loss is heavier than ever. We have but 136 men for duty. Please accept this gift in remembrance of us and our suffering comrades.

W. H——, Sergeant.
J. F——, Corporal.

The Sergeant received his commission, was wounded again before Richmond, recovered, was mustered out with his regiment at the close of the war, and wrote to me that he was on his way to the Rocky Mountains to seek his fortune. I have no doubt that he will find it.

The Superintendent's "Service of Plate"

O NE MORNING after a large number of Soldiers had been returned to duty, this letter without name was found in the post-office box at the store-room door:

MISS ——

These few imperfect lines are designed to express the gratitude of one of the many grateful hearts indebted to you, by the many kind words and deeds you have bestowed on us, the sick and wounded soldiers of this Hospital. When in your presence we find it impossible to express our thankfulness, and fearing that you may think us incapable of appreciating your kindness, and in justice to our own hearts, I have, with the approval of my comrades, resolved to try to communicate to you some little evidence of our regard. Though I am confident my poor pen will not do our feelings justice, still I hope to be able to convince you that the soldiers sometimes think of you and are not forgetful of your kindness. The many expressions of sympathy and encouragement that have dropped from your lips are treasured up and prized by us with reverence and honorable pride. We know that to you we are indebted for many of the comforts and good things we enjoy here. Please accept this acknowledgment of our gratitude, with the assurance that if our prayers are answered, your journey of life will be one of uninterrupted happiness and prosperity, and your final reward such as God only can bestow.

I am very respectfully,
ONE OF MANY SOLDIERS.

Last Days

T HE LAST FEW MONTHS OF HOSPITAL LIFE WERE full of excitement and toil. There was great rejoicing when the news came that Richmond was fallen and the war ended. Thunder and smoke ran at once round all the circle of the forts; an improvised salute without orders, and pistol-snapping, shouts and music filled the air. The men moved about in little squads, in marching time, singing by snatches, "Rally round the Flag," and

> *"The star-spangled banner in triumph shall wave,*
> *O'er the land of the Free and Jeff Davis his grave."*

Certain of the cripples hobbled out of the barracks, turned southward, and long and solemnly waved and brandished their crutches in the air. It seemed to do them good. At night the city was illuminated, and we saw from the tower the long lines of buildings and the great dome pricked out in light upon the dark-blue distance, and the red glare of the joy-fires reflected in the sky.

Presently a large number of wounded men, the men who had taken Richmond, came up on the steamers and kept us very busy for a time. It was delightful to work for these men. Their spirit was magnificent. The tide was at the full. The rush to break all bounds and get home had not yet begun. "You have left one foot for the rebels?" "Oh yes, the rebels have got it, but then you know Richmond's gone up." "It was your right arm?" "Yes, but the war is over and the country is saved; they might have had the other arm if they had wanted it;" and, "so say we all of us!" half sang, half shouted all the maimed men within hearing. The little groups about the doors were always breaking into hurrahs on the slightest occasion or allusion.

Very coldly on the thunder and the shouting fell the dark April morning on which a vague rumor of the Tragedy in the city crept through the camp like a deadly, chilling fog. A trivial matter made the rumor known at first. John came to the store-room to say that the market wagons were turned back from the outer guard, and the special diet supplies had not come; that no milkcarts or mail riders had got through; that "*something*" must have happened. By degrees, no one knew how or whence, the story came; a darker and darker version every hour. We believed nothing, till the Surgeon in Charge passed the guard as a medical officer, went to headquarters in the nearest town, and, after two or three hours' delay, got back with authentic information.

Hard work was a blessing in those cold and heavy hours; all our expedients with reserves of canned meats and soups were called into use; no supplies came out for a day or two; every house and hut in the neighborhood was surrounded and searched, and comers and goers were sharply questioned.

How the sun shone and how loud the birds sang on that Easter Sunday! I remember the keen impression made by little things. I can smell the lilacs now. In intervals of work when we sat down to rest we sat with folded hands, looking at each other in silence. The men came with streaming tears to ask for bits of crape and ribbon to fasten on their sleeves. "It's with me, night and day," they say, "I can't sleep for thinking,"—"If it had been my own brother;" and the roughest of all contraband women in the quarters, drawing the back of her hand across her eyes says: "Oh Missis! I feel like as if my own kin was gone."

On Easter Monday the Chaplain went to a meeting of ministers of the District and the whole body waited on Mr. Johnson at the Treasury Building. The President replied with apparent emotion to the address and resolutions, saying in closing: "The American people need to be educated to see that treason is a crime."

On the Funeral Day the chapel was crowded for the solemn service. We had, unhappily, black shawls and crape veils enough among us, and the pulpit and chancel were hung with the soft, dark folds. The men all wore tokens of mourning. There was not a contraband hut in all the fields between the Hospital and the city but had its poor little rag of black above the door.

Homeward coming troops began to arrive in the neighborhood. First came the Ninth Corps and spread their tents just beyond our fields, and soon on every slope and ridge about us lay the camps of Sherman and of the Army of the Potomac, musical by day, smoky and twinkling by night, picturesque always. From the tower top in the twilight we saw low belts of smoke marking the line of "watch-fires of a thousand circling camps," and all day long we heard the shouts and the brass-music. Squads of sick men came in, hourly, from all the outlying regiments, some in ambulance trains, some wearily creeping up on foot;—measles, chronic diarrhoea, typho-malarial fever;—men dragged about with their regiments, some in the third week of fever, came in speechless or wandering and died just after getting on a clean bed. This was the "grand march home."

Convalescents from among these men and the men from the camps thronged the store-room all day long. The tower was a beacon; one said to another: "Do you see that 'cupalo'? There's a sanitary up there"; and as far as the stores held out they were gladly given to all, the Hospital inmates of course having the first choice. "Sherman's men" were generally tall, loose-hung, handsome fellows, and wore the slouch hat and bit of feather. The Eastern men wore the trimmer foraging cap and were shorter and more compactly built. East and West "chaffed" each other now and then, but on the whole there was very little friction and a great deal of brotherliness.

The patients who came to us were many of them very ill, thoroughly worn out; we had scores of cases of malignant fever besides other camp diseases; they came weary, broken down, dusty, ragged, and what I never saw before, barefoot. This was the "grand march home."

It was a keen pleasure to supply these men with shirts, socks, slippers for their travel-sore feet, tobacco, books, anything. In the wards it was good to see the brightness go up and down the lines of beds, following the plentiful supplies of illustrated papers and magazines. "'The Atlantic?' Oh yes ! I always used to read it." "Just let me see that 'Harper.' My folks always took that, but it's three years since I saw a copy." "Dear me, this is just what we all want to *rest* us." "Did you really get those turkeys, boys, on the march to the sea?" "Oh no'm," they laughed. "We had our marching rations and were satisfied with them."

Up to the store-room one morning, among others crept W——, a Swiss from Wisconsin, meagre, shrivelled, and ragged, and looking twenty years older than his age. He came to see if he could get some blackberry syrup and a handkerchief, pulling out a rag of what had been a handkerchief once. "We were two brothers"—this was is little story; "I had no wife; he had a wife and children. I said I could go better than he; one must go; so I went. I have been marching I think almost without rest for nearly a year, marching and fighting; hard and heavy marches they were. But it is over now; *the country is safe*, and perhaps I shall get well in Wisconsin. (Alas! he would never get well.) At any rate there is a God who takes care 'over' us all. *At Chattanooga I saw God.* I had but heard of Him before; I shall see Him always, now."

The men did not like the Great Review. "They say Grant means to march us through Pennsylvania Avenue with our trains, about fifty miles of 'em. There may be people who like to see army trains; I don't." It was very warm; two or three men came in with sunstroke about that time; one and all scolded about the Great Review. But when the day came all wanted to go as spectators at least, and the Hospital was half emptied of men and officers. No one abused the furlough. There was but little drunkenness or confusion among our own men, and wonderfully little among the regiments lying about us. One provisional division made up of odd regiments and bits of regiments was a noisy, uneasy, turbulent throng. There was universal anxiety to break up and get home, but the men showed more patience and composure than many of their officers.

We mustered out and discharged constantly, and constantly received new patients. We took in fourteen hundred and ninety in the last fortnight of May, and were obliged to care for them with make-shift wardmasters and "emergency" cooks. Every one wanted to go. Every one who had any claim to go was released at once by the Surgeon in Charge, who was carefully just and patient with those who went and those who stayed behind. Order 116 from the Adjutant General's office, mustering out all Veteran Reserves whose original regiments had gone home, made great confusion and trouble. It took every printer, every clerk from the office, every cook but one,—head nurses, wardmasters, and commisionary sergeants. The only gleam of satisfaction was that it took the latest store-room orderly, the third in ten days, a dreadful boy, who being sent into the next room to weigh stores comes back with cheeks smeared with sweetmeats and mouth crammed with cheese, and asks mumbling, "Whodgerwantdonethemeggs?" and brings in notes opening and reading them on the way and saying: "Oh! here's into *you* about the punch!" Office business had come nearly to a stand-still, for the Surgeon in Charge, though he wrote all day and all night, could no more make out all the papers than the Superintendent could do all the cooking, when "as much of 116 A. G. O. as relates to men of the Second Battalion," was rescinded. Meantime more than half these men had gone or were in process of going, and those who were obliged to remain could hardly be appeased, believing themselves victims of some injustice.

We had at this season plenty of fresh vegetables, the sweetest and greenest of green peas, string beans, etc., from the Hospital garden. Those who doubt the possibility of extracting sunbeams from cucumbers should see the effect of this and other vegetables in the convalescent's wards. We had, later, small fruits and peaches enough for the more delicate men. The new store-room orderly, the fourth in two weeks, having a bushel of peaches to pare and cut up for dinner, begins at nine o'clock and at eleven applies for another man to help him.

In an interval of work we went over to some of the field hospitals, and found the same old story,—measles, chronic diarrhoea, typhoid fever and pork and beans; nothing else; not even soft bread, except in one place where there was some yellow slush being shaken about in a battered can in the smoke of the trench-fire; this I was told was "fariny." Three or four men in this hospital were very low. "Couldn't they send them to us or to town?" "No; wanted 'em on the rolls." They were off the rolls next morning.

In the last days of June came the circular from the Sanitary Commission saying that its Field and Hospital Relief service was finished,—written across in pencil—

> *For now the whole Round Table is dissolved,*
> *The old order changes, yielding place to new,*
> *And God fulfill Himself in many way.*
> *Pray for my soul. More things are wrought by prayer*
> *Than this world dreams of.* * * *
> * * * Something ere the end,*
> *Some work of noble note may yet be done*
> *Not unbecoming men that strove with gods.*

Transfers and discharges thinned the Hospital ranks. Two hundred and ninety men went in one day. Wardmasters and cooks, "emergency men," disappeared among them, and it was very difficult to get through the day's work for the sixty to a hundred special diet patients on the returns in July. Volunteer labor was never more needed. The men who remained in the wards required more care, and, owing to the general disorganization, got less from the regular sources than ever before. Day by day we dissolved; night by night the camps about us vanished. The slopes of the near hills, all twinkling and musical one evening, were on the next almost savagely silent and lonely.

We saw now and then an ugly feature of the general disbanding. Private S., after the most careful and tender nursing, was discharged one day and came back the next night robbed of his pay, quite tipsy and with a new and dishonorable wound in his arm. It was found that another discharged man had carried with him, besides his Sanitary Commission comforts, a beautiful saddle, a Christmas present from the medical officers to the Surgeon in Charge.

Men with the noses

"Peculiar to persons named Levy and Moses"

hung about the camp waiting for their "friends." Regimental officers wrote ignorant and injudicious notes to their men, telling them they were "musterd out already and kneed n't stay a day longer in Hospital if able to travil." We were occasionally imposed on, no doubt, in issuing articles from the store-room, in spite of precautions on all sides, for old Mrs. B—— came more than once to report, with characteristic twitch of the nose, that "more of them destitute men were a wantin' packin' boxes to send their things home." All but a faithful few shirked work and grumbled. These, though they will not see these pages, I thank from my heart once more. These few—surgeons, nurses, and wardmasters—worked, weary but unfaltering, day and night, and parted sadly at last, interchanging little trifles of remembrance and "sorrowing most of all that they should see each other's faces no more."

The last of July the final order came: "You are directed to say how soon your Hospital can be emptied, property packed, and place turned over," etc. The Surgeon in Charge, being a prodigious worker, answered: "In ten days." Those ten days were very laborious. The fatigues of all were aggravated by the intense heat. Five weeks of torrid weather, with hotter nights than days, had ended in a terrific wind-and-rain-storm, during which chimneys crashed through the roofs and trees were violently twisted out of the ground. Two or three price-less cool days followed, and then the terrible August heats set in again. Early in that month the Sixteenth New York Heavy Artillery encamped in our grove, very glad, poor fellows, to come down from the bare and blazing ridge they had been spread over, very glad to have the last letter-paper, handker-chiefs and towels from the store-room, and expressing their acknowledgments in the usual manner, through the band.

All the Hospital goods were packed and boxed, and daily wagon-trains went down the hill carrying the "property" to the city; the last of the sick were taken over—one man in his bed—to a city hospital, and in the middle of August the quar-termaster made his last inspecting tour, with a paper in his hand in which the fugitive owners of the place asked that the Secretary of War would "Restore the buildings, cause thor-ough repairs to be made, and pay a proper rent for the time they had been occupied by the Government."

In the still, fresh summer dawn we drove for the last time through the grove, down the long winding road to the high-way leading to the city. The camp was silent and desolate, the store-room was empty and bare, the wards were quarter-master's lumber. Behind us the tower stood black against gray trailing clouds. Low flights of birds went circling round and round it. Before us the great dome showed spectral in the vapors of a sunrise that struggled and did not shine.

Related Books from Edinborough Press

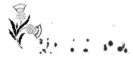

Three Weeks at Gettysburg
by Georgeanna Woolsey Bacon

Georgeanna Woolsey, the sister of the author of *Hospital Days*, served as a nurse throughout the Civil War. Following the Battle of Gettysburg, she tended to the wounded for three weeks. This essay was written to promote the efforts of the U.S. Sanitary Commission.

ISBN 0-889020-02-8

Price: $2.95   32 pages   Soft cover

The Brothers
A Story of the Massachusetts Fifty–fourth Regiment
by Louisa May Alcott

Alcott served as a nurse, gathering many stories into her book, *Hospital Sketches*. This short story, written for a popular magazine of the day, gives a fictional account of the heroics of the Massachusetts 54th Regiment.

ISBN 0-889020-01-X

Price: $2.95   32 pages   Soft cover

To order, write:

Edinborough Press
P.O. Box 13790
Roseville, MN 55113–2293

Please include $1.75 for shipping and handling.
Minnesota residents, please include sales tax.